bluejean

C H E F

Air Fry GENIUS

Meredith Laurence

Photography by Jessica Walker

Walah!, LLC Publishers
Philadelphia

First Edition

Published in the United States by Walah!, LLC/Publishers

walah@me.com

Publisher's Cataloging-In-Publication Data
(Prepared by The Donohue Group, Inc.)

Names: Laurence, Meredith. | Walker, Jessica, 1975- photographer.
Title: Air fry genius / Meredith Laurence ; photography by Jessica Walker.
Description: First edition. | Philadelphia : Walah!, LLC Publishers, [2017] | "Blue Jean Chef." | Includes index.
Identifiers: ISBN 978-0-9827540-6-1 | ISBN 0-9827540-6-X
Subjects: LCSH: Hot air frying. | LCGFT: Cookbooks.
Classification: LCC TX689 .L38 2017 | DDC 641.7/7--dc23

Printed in USA

Book design by Janis Boehm
www.bound-determined.com

Photography by Jessica Walker
www.jessicawalkerphotography.com

Food styling by Lisa Martin

Acknowledgments

I have an amazing team that worked with me to put this book together and I truly couldn't have done it without them. What amazes me is that I'm able to call all these people my friends. I am the luckiest. Thank you. Thank you. Thank you!

To my right hand, Lisa Martin... Thank you for all your support and help. From recipes to photos, you are a skilled planner and a true leader in the food styling world. How great it is to be able to work so hard with someone and still laugh all the time.

To my designer, Janis Boehm... You are my most patient friend. I so enjoy working with you, even down to the wire. We always see eye-to-eye and you seem to know what I'm thinking before I do. Thank you for that and for your eye for design.

To my photographer, Jessica Walker... Spending so much quality time with you just might be a good enough reason to write another book. Thank you for your beautiful photos, for your friendship and for great conversations over many long days.

To my amazing food styling team – Bill Hornaday, Lucille Osborn, Michele Pilone and Lori Phelan. You did beautiful work and were all such a pleasure to have around. I miss our morning meetings and family meals.

To my editing and proof-reading team... Not just any friends would, or could do what you did. Tanya van Biesen, Suzanne Smith and especially Penny Markowitz who must have read this book more times than anyone ever will!.

To Linda Lisco... You are definitely in my corner. There's a fine line between consulting and counseling. I'm very grateful you do both.

To Amy Nichols... Your adept handling of the printing side of the business and keeping the train on the tracks is forever appreciated.

To Eric Theiss... My wall to lean on for so many years now. Thank you for always being there.

To my family, Annie, Ruby and Hazel. You bring sunshine to my life every day. Thank you for putting up with my rainy days and making the sun shine through.

Table of Contents

Table of Contents

Foreword
by David Venable

Meredith has done it again! She has gone back into the kitchen to whip up a sequel to her first air frying cookbook, *Air Fry Everything!*, and has come to the table with *Air Fry Genius*. This collection of over 100 new dishes can be prepared using the oh-so-versatile and popular air fryer. Staying true to her roots as a home-cooking instructor, Meredith helps us understand, in simple terms, how an air fryer can change the way we cook—ultimately making fast, creative dishes that use little or no oil.

Every recipe is mouthwatering, but I have to call out a few at the top of my list. Fried Cheese Ravioli with Marinara Sauce, Simple Buttermilk Fried Chicken, and Pork Taco Gorditas have me putting my grocery list together. I'm also thrilled with the idea of Air Fried Roast Beef with Rosemary Potatoes, a Garlic Parmesan Bread Ring, and of course, Teriyaki Chicken Drumsticks.

While the savory dishes are incredible, Meredith also delivers delicious desserts! Check out recipes such as her Peanut Butter Cup Doughnut Holes, S'mores Pockets, and Air Fried Strawberry Hand Tarts. Also, don't miss the Hassleback Apple Crisp, Annie's Chocolate Chunk Hazelnut Cookies, and the decadent Midnight Nutella Banana Sandwich. I can feel the Happy Dances starting already!

Finally, each of the easy-to-follow recipes comes with a beautiful color photo to help us see and realize how the finished dishes should look. Meredith even provides the nutritional information so we can make decisions that are good for every appetite. I especially appreciate her tips, simple rules, and conversions, allowing all of us to become accomplished air fryers.

Let this cookbook—and your air fryer—lead the way to flavorful food that your family and friends will be talking about long after the meal is over. Enjoy!

David Venable
Host of QVC's *In the Kitchen with David*®

Introduction

"I use my air fryer for everything!"

I often hear that phrase from many of my readers and it makes me so happy. That was exactly what I wanted people to get out of my first air fryer cookbook, Air Fry Everything! You really can use your air fryer for (well... almost) everything. The message was received loud and clear and I was thrilled. Air Fry Everything! sold over 200,000 copies and people jumped onto the air fryer train, realizing its potential to not only replicate deep-fried foods, but to cook stovetop and oven meals as well, all with less fat but just as much flavor.

Since then, I've continued to cook with my air fryer, almost every day. It's become an essential part of my kitchen. I use it for everything from toasting nuts as an ingredient, to making a quick "grilled" sandwich for lunch, to creating less guilt-ridden indulgences, to full dinners and of course, delicious decadent desserts. It's easy, quick, clean and effective and I love it. So, of course it has been fun for me to learn even more about this brilliant appliance and discover all its genius features.

That brings me to this book – Air Fry Genius. This time around, I'm continuing to give you a variety of dishes, from snacks to desserts, but I'm also letting you in on all the secrets that I've learned about air-frying. You can read more about these secrets on page 16 under Genius Discoveries and throughout the book in all the new recipes.

If you've been riding the air fryer train with me so far, I hope you're excited about the journey ahead. If you're new to air frying, welcome aboard. I'm thrilled to have you along!

If You are Brand New to Air Frying

Air Frying Basics

In the simplest of terms, an air-fryer is a compact cylindrical countertop convection oven. It's a kitchen appliance that uses superheated air to cook foods, giving results very similar to deep-frying or high-temperature roasting. Convection cooking is not new to the culinary world. Many of us have convection ovens (or a convection setting) in our kitchens, where the air is heated by an element and then blown around by a fan. This creates more energy and consequently cooks foods faster and more evenly. Air fryers use the same technology as convection ovens, but instead of blowing the air around a large rectangular box, it is blown around in a compact cylinder and the food sits in a perforated basket. This is much more efficient and creates an intense environment of heat from which the food cannot escape. The result is food with a crispy brown exterior and moist tender interior – results similar to deep-frying, but without all the oil and fat needed to deep-fry. In fact, when you air-fry, you usually use no more than one tablespoon of oil!

Better still, an air fryer doesn't just cook foods that you would usually deep-fry. It can cook any foods that you would normally roast, bake, grill, sauté or even microwave. It is a great tool for re-heating foods without making them rubbery, and is a perfect and quick way to prepare ingredients as well as make meals. It has become a valued helper in my kitchen.

Health Benefits

Obviously, because it can produce results similar to deep-frying using a tiny fraction of the oil needed to deep-fry, the health benefits are apparent. When deep-frying, you submerge the food in oil and oil is inevitably absorbed by the food. In an air fryer, you still use oil because oil is what helps crisp and brown many foods, but you really don't need more than one tablespoon at a time. Instead of putting the tablespoon of oil in the air fryer, you simply toss foods with oil and then place them in the air fryer basket. In fact, spraying the foods lightly with oil is an even easier way to get foods evenly coated with the least amount of oil. Investing in a kitchen spray bottle is a great idea if you have an air fryer.

Quick and Energy Efficient

Pre-heating a standard oven can take fifteen to twenty minutes. An air fryer, on the other hand, can pre-heat in two or three minutes because of its compact size. That's a huge savings in time as well as energy. In the summer, you can pre-heat your air fryer and not heat up the whole kitchen. In addition, the intense heat created in the air fryer cooks foods quickly, about 20% faster than in an oven, so you're saving time and energy there as well. Saving time makes for happier cooks!

Safe and Easy to Use

Air-frying is safer and easier than deep-frying. Most air fryers have settings for time and temperature. You simply enter both and press start. It doesn't get much easier than that! When deep-frying, you have to heat a large pot of oil on the stovetop, use a deep-frying thermometer to register the temperature and then monitor the heat below the pot to maintain that temperature. On top of that, you are dealing with a lot of oil, which can be heavy to move, dangerous if it gets too hot, and is cumbersome and annoying to drain and dispose of. Why bother if you can use an air fryer to get the same delicious results?

Clean and Tidy

I'm a tidy cook! I love keeping the kitchen clean and neat when I'm cooking and after I've been cooking. The air fryer fits into my world perfectly. It cooks foods in a contained space and consequently eliminates splatter in the kitchen. Period. It is simple and straightforward to clean and keep clean, and you know what they say about cleanliness... 😊

Using Air Fryers to Prepare Ingredients

So often, I find myself turning to the air fryer to cook ingredients for meals that might not even call for an air fryer. Don't underestimate the convenience of quickly toasting some nuts for a salad, or roasting a pepper for pasta, or quickly cooking bacon for an egg sandwich. Ingredients in recipes often come with a qualifier – "walnuts, toasted", or "bread cubes, toasted" – and the air fryer comes to the rescue, once again saving precious time.

Genius Discoveries

In writing and testing so many recipes and after making so many meals in the air fryer, I've discovered a few nuances to air-frying that really make a difference to getting the most out of your new favorite kitchen appliance. I've discovered ways to take advantage of all that an air fryer has to offer, as well as overcome some of its shortcomings. I call these genius discoveries and in this book, I'm letting you in on these secrets.

- **Use your air fryer as a proof box.** Proofing is an important step in making yeast dough – allowing the dough to rest and rise in a warm moist environment. You can create the perfect warm moist environment with your air fryer. Pour 1 cup of water in the bottom drawer of the air fryer and then pre-heat it to 400°F for several minutes. Place the dough (in an oiled bowl) in the turned off fryer basket and it can sit there to rise perfectly until you're ready to use it. You'll see this technique used for many of the dough recipes in the book, from the Garlic Parmesan Bread Ring on page 59 to the Peach Fritters on page 76.

- **Add water to the air fryer drawer when cooking fatty foods.** One of the great benefits of an air fryer with a perforated basket is that fat from foods will drain through the basket and into the drawer below, away from the food itself. The only trouble with this is that if the cooking time is of any significance, the grease can get too hot and smoke. Adding water to the drawer underneath the basket helps prevent the grease from smoking. I do this when I make the Peppered Maple Bacon Knots on page 82, the Bourbon Bacon Burgers on page 104 and even the Hasselback Apple Crisp on page 244, which has butter that drips down below the basket.

- **Use toothpicks to hold foods down.** Every once in a while, the fan from the air fryer will pick up light foods and blow them around. So, secure foods (like the top slice of bread on a sandwich, or a slice of cheese on top of a burger) with toothpicks.

- **Add water to the air fryer to create a moist cooking environment.** Because air fryers work by blowing hot air around, they create a very dry cooking environment. They keep foods moist because they cook so efficiently that there's not enough time for the food to dry out. There are some foods, however, that need a lower temperature and a little more time in order to become tender. With these foods, a moist cooking environment is needed. The good news is that there is a way to create a moist environment in the air fryer by adding liquid to the bottom drawer. I do this when cooking the Blackberry BBQ Glazed Country-Style Ribs on page 130. The ribs need a lower temperature and more time to tenderize and putting a little sherry or Madeira wine in the bottom helps create the needed moisture and imparts some flavor too. The same technique is used on the lobster tails on page 190.

- **Use an aluminum foil sling**. Any oven-safe pan is also air-fryer-safe, which now allows you to bake foods that are made in cake pans. The only challenge in using these accessories is actually getting them into and out of the air fryer basket. To make it easier, fold a piece of aluminum foil into a strip about 2-inches wide by 24-inches long. Place the cake pan or baking dish on the foil and by holding the ends of the foil, you'll be able to lift the pan or dish and lower it into the air fryer basket. Fold or tuck the ends of the aluminum foil into the air fryer basket, and then return the basket to the air fryer. When you're ready to remove the pan, unfold and hold onto the ends of the aluminum foil to lift the pan out of the air fryer basket. I use this technique a lot and you'll see it throughout the book.

- **Elevate foods for better browning.** This technique replicates broiling in your oven and gives you extra browning when you really want it. You can use a rack accessory to elevate the foods in the air fryer basket, or an inverted air-fryer-safe dish, or you can even make your own rack using crumpled up aluminum foil. When I was making the T-bone steak on page 90, I really wanted some good browning and charring on the surface of the steak. Elevating it with some aluminum foil in the basket did the trick. The same technique works for caramelizing the sugar in the Brown Sugar Grapefruit on page 84.

- **Using the basket as a meatloaf pan.** The best meatloaf pans are perforated, allowing grease to drip away from the meat as it cooks. Many air fryers have a similar design with their perforated baskets, which allows you to use the basket as a built-in meatloaf pan. The only tricks you need to know are to put some water in the bottom drawer to prevent the grease from smoking, and to use a spatula to pull the meatloaf away from the sides of the basket – just so air can more easily surround the meatloaf. This is all described on page 110 in the recipe for Meatloaf with Tangy Tomato Glaze.

- **Don't pour away the juices from the drawer too soon.** The drawer below the air fryer basket collects a lot of juices from the cooked foods above and catches any marinades that you pour over the food. If the drippings are not too greasy, you can use this flavorful liquid as a sauce to pour over the food. You can also de-grease this liquid and reduce it in a small saucepan on the stovetop for a few minutes to concentrate the flavor.

- **"Slow cooking" in the air fryer.** I wouldn't have thought it possible, but you can actually cook more slowly in an air fryer too. Most air fryers have a low temperature range around 200°F. This allows you to cook foods gently over longer periods of time. In the Beef and Spinach Braciole recipe on page 99, you put the rolled and stuffed beef in a cake pan with tomato sauce, cover it and let it slow cook at 250°F for an hour. No need to turn on your oven!

- **Cooking en Papillotte.** Cooking fish "en papillotte", or wrapped in parchment paper, is one of my favorite ways to cook fish. It allows you to cook the fish and make a sauce all at the same time. You can do this in your air fryer as well. Paper ignites at 451°F, but most air fryers only go as high as 400°F so that is not a problem. Wrap the fish in the parchment with some flavorful ingredients and a little wine and butter and pop it into your air fryer basket. If you wrap it properly and nothing leaks out, you won't even have to wash up the air fryer at the end! You'll see this technique in the Salmon Puttanesca en Papillotte with Zucchini on page 174.

- **Cheese melter.** An air fryer will retain some of its temperature after you've turned it off. This is a perfect opportunity to use the air fryer as a cheese melter. If you're topping your food with cheese, just slide it back into the turned off air fryer and there will be enough residual heat to melt that cheese perfectly.

General Tips for Air-Frying

Preparing to air-fry

- **Find the right place for your air fryer in your kitchen.** Always keep your air fryer on a level, heat-resistant countertop and make sure there are at least five inches of space behind the air fryer where the exhaust vent is located.

- **Pre-heat your air fryer before adding your food.** This is easy – just turn the air fryer on to the temperature that you need and set the timer for 2 or 3 minutes. When the timer goes off, the air fryer has pre-heated and is ready for food.

- **Invest in a kitchen spray bottle.** Spraying oil on the food is easier than drizzling or brushing, and allows you to use less oil overall. While you can buy oil sprays in cans, sometimes there are aerosol agents in those cans that can break down the non-stick surface on your air fryer basket. So, if you want to spray foods directly in the basket, invest in a hand-pumped kitchen spray bottle. It will be worth it!

- **Get the right accessories.** Once you start air frying, you may want to invest in some accessories for your new favorite appliance. Truth is, you may already have some! Any baking dishes or cake pans that are oven-safe should be air fryer-safe as well, as long as they don't come in contact with the heating element. The only stipulation, of course, is that the accessory pan has to be able to fit inside the air fryer basket.

While you are air-frying

- **Don't overcrowd the basket.** I can't stress this enough. It's tempting to try to cook more at one time, but over-crowding the basket will prevent foods from crisping and browning evenly and take more time over all.

- **Flip foods over halfway through the cooking time.** Just as you would if you were cooking on a grill or in a skillet, you need to turn foods over so that they brown evenly.

- **Open the air fryer as often as you like to check for doneness.** This is one of the best parts of air fryers – you can open that drawer as often as you like (within reason) to check to see how the cooking process is coming along. This will not interrupt the timing of most air fryers – the fryer will either continue heating and timing as you pull the basket out, or pick up where it left off when you return the basket to the fryer.

- **Shake the basket.** Shaking the basket a couple of times during the cooking process will re-distribute the ingredients and help them to brown and crisp more evenly.

- **Spray with oil part way through.** If you are trying to get the food to brown and crisp more, try spritzing it with oil part way through the cooking process. This will also help the food to brown more evenly.

After you air-fry

- **Remove the air fryer basket from the drawer before turning out foods.** This is very important and it's a mistake you'll only make once. If you invert the basket while it is still locked into the air fryer drawer, you will end up dumping all the rendered fat or excess grease onto your plate along with the food you just air-fried.

- **Clean the drawer as well as the basket after every use.** The drawer of the air fryer is very easy to clean, so don't put it off. If you leave it unwashed, you'll run the risk of food contamination and your kitchen won't smell very nice in a day or so!

- **Use the air fryer to dry itself.** After washing the air fryer basket and drawer, just pop them back into the air fryer and turn it on for 2 or 3 minutes. That dries both parts better than any drying towel.

Re-heating foods in the air-fryer

- There's no hard and fast rule for time and temperature when re-heating leftovers because leftovers vary so significantly. I suggest re-heating in the air fryer at 350°F and doing so for as long as it takes for the food to be re-heated to a food safety temperature of 165°F. This is especially important for any potentially hazardous foods like chicken, pork and beef.

Trouble-shooting

- **Food is not getting crispy enough.** Make sure you are not over-crowding the air fryer basket and make sure you are using a little oil.

- **There is white smoke coming from the air fryer.** Add some water to the air fryer drawer underneath the basket. The white smoke is probably because grease has drained into the drawer and is burning. Adding water will prevent this.

- **There is black smoke coming from the air fryer.** Turn the machine off and look up towards the heating element inside the fryer. Some food might have blown up and attached to the heating element, burning and causing the black smoke.

- **The air fryer won't turn off.** Many air fryers are designed to have a delay in their shutting down process. Once you press the power button off, the fan will continue to blow the hot air out of the unit for about 20 seconds. Don't press the power button again, or you will have just turned the machine back on. Be patient and wait, and the air fryer will turn off.

Nutritional Information

While air-frying is healthier for you than many other cooking methods, deep-frying in particular, this cookbook does not in any way present itself as a diet or lifestyle cookbook. I've included nutritional information for every recipe in large part because of reader requests. Many of us read nutritional labels these days, but there are as many reasons for doing so as there are those of us who do! Some of us watch calories, others watch fat content, some are looking at cholesterol and others are trying to avoid sugar. Some of the recipes in this book are low in calories; others are not. Some are low in fat; others are not. I've given you the information so that you can be informed and decide what it is you want to eat. I don't believe in strict diets (unless they are medically advised), but I am a proponent of moderation. I won't eat a Midnight Nutella® Banana Sandwich (page 257) *every* day, but every once in a while, I'll indulge. So, use the nutritional information as it suits you. Below are a few points to help you understand the numbers.

- **Compare air-frying to the traditional cooking technique.** Obviously, when air-frying is replacing deep-frying as the cooking technique, there is a much lower amount of oil required and consumed. When you are air-frying instead of roasting or sautéing, you will also consume less fat because any excess fat from meats will drip through the air fryer basket and away from your food. However, when you are air-frying instead of baking, there is no nutritional advantage to using the air fryer and the nutritional values will be the same.

- **Sodium.** I have not included sodium values in the recipes because I cannot give you a reliable measurement. Every recipe should be seasoned to taste and everyone's taste varies. If you are on a low-sodium diet, I suggest you add no salt at all, but try to rely on spices and seasonings and sodium replacements instead.

- **Serving Size.** Some of the recipes in the book have a serving range – "Serves 4 to 6", for example. In these instances, the nutritional values will apply to the larger serving suggestion (or the smaller portion) – dividing the recipe into 6 servings, in this instance.

- **Gluten free.** Recipes that are gluten free have become a prized commodity for those suffering from gluten sensitivities. You will find all recipes that are gluten free *or have an easy way to become gluten free* marked as such in the book. This is marked by a *GF* or *GF** in the side bar and I hope it is helpful.

Converting Recipes to Your Air Fryer

Converting From Traditional Recipes

You can use your air fryer to cook recipes that have instructions for cooking in the oven. Because the heat in the air fryer is more intense than a standard oven, reduce the suggested temperature by 25°F – 50°F and cut the time by roughly 20%. So, if a recipe calls for cooking at 400°F for 20 minutes, air-fry at 370°F for about 16 minutes. You can also refer to the cooking charts in this book on page 270 to help determine the right cooking time for foods. Remember to turn foods over halfway through the cooking time (as you would in a skillet or on the grill) and check the foods for your desired degree of doneness as you approach the finish line.

Converting From Packaged Foods Instructions

The same rule applies to prepared foods that you might buy at the grocery store. If a bag of frozen French fries suggests cooking in the oven at 450°F for 18 minutes, air fry the fries at 400°F and start checking them at 15 minutes, remembering to shake the basket once or twice during the cooking process to help the fries brown evenly.

Converting to Different Sized Air-Fryers

The recipes in this book were tested with various various brands and wattages of 3-quart air fryers. If you are using an air fryer that is larger than 3-quarts, then you're in luck. Larger air fryers can make life a little easier, especially if you're cooking for 4 or more people. Because the baskets in these air fryers are larger, you can cook more food at one time and do not have to cook the food in batches as specified in many of these recipes. In addition, you might also find that you can shave a few minutes off the cooking time. Just remember not to over-fill the air fryer basket, since that will just slow down the overall cooking time and result in foods that are not as crispy as you'd like them to be. As with all things you cook in the air fryer, it makes sense to pull open the air fryer drawer and check the foods as they cook. That way, you'll avoid over-cooking anything.

If you are using an air fryer that is smaller than 3-quarts, don't fret. You can still make most of the recipes in this cookbook – you'll just do smaller batches at one time. The only recipes that won't be possible are the larger roast recipes – turkey breast, whole roast chicken or roast beef – unless you get a smaller chicken or roast that you can fit into your air fryer basket.

Regardless of what size air fryer you are using, understand that much like cooking in an oven or on the stovetop, timing may vary a little based on a number of factors – the size of your food (large chicken breasts versus smaller chicken breasts), the size of the cuts of foods, the temperature of your ingredients, etc... Use your better judgment when cooking to determine when foods are cooked to your liking. The great thing about an air fryer is that you can very easily remove the drawer at any time during the cooking process to see how things are going.

If you would like to learn more about air-frying, or would like more recipes for your air-fryer and other cooking tools, please visit me at **www.bluejeanchef.com**.

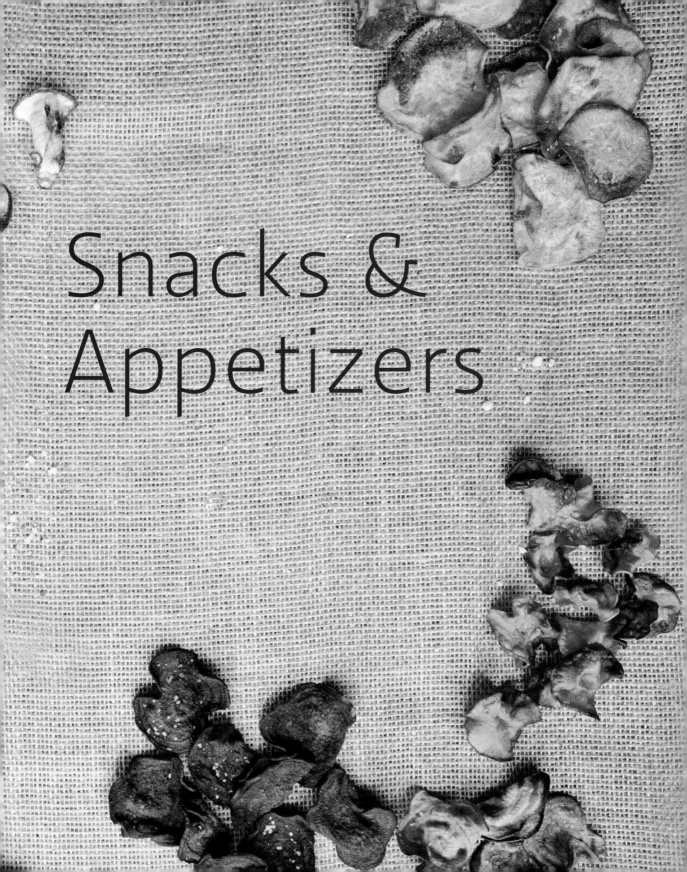

Snacks & Appetizers

Cauliflower "Tater" Tots

Serves: **6 to 8** ▪ Temperature: **400˚F** ▪ Cooking Time: **10 minutes per batch**

Veg
GF*

1 head of cauliflower

2 eggs

¼ cup all-purpose flour*

½ cup grated Parmesan cheese

1 teaspoon salt

freshly ground black pepper

vegetable or olive oil, in a spray bottle

*Make this recipe gluten free by using a gluten-free flour.

1. Grate the head of cauliflower with a box grater or finely chop it in a food processor. You should have about 3½ cups. Place the chopped cauliflower in the center of a clean kitchen towel and twist the towel tightly to squeeze all the water out of the cauliflower. (This can be done in two batches to make it easier to drain all the water from the cauliflower.)

2. Place the squeezed cauliflower in a large bowl. Add the eggs, flour, Parmesan cheese, salt and freshly ground black pepper. Shape the cauliflower into small cylinders or "tater tot" shapes, rolling roughly one tablespoon of the mixture at a time. Place the tots on a cookie sheet lined with paper towel to absorb any residual moisture. Spray the cauliflower tots all over with oil.

3. Pre-heat the air fryer to 400°F.

4. Air-fry the tots at 400°F, one layer at a time for 10 minutes, turning them over for the last few minutes of the cooking process for even browning. Season with salt and black pepper. Serve hot with your favorite dipping sauce.

Make it Ahead

These little tots freeze really well, so you can make them well in advance. Freeze them raw on a cookie sheet and then proceed with steps 3 and 4 when you're ready. You can also freeze them after they have been air-fried and just re-heat them in your air fryer at 350°F for 6 minutes. If you would like this snack a little cheesier, substitute grated Cheddar cheese for the Parmesan cheese. Yum!

Per Serving 80 Calories – 3g Fat (1g Sat. Fat) – 55mg Cholesterol – 8g Carbohydrates – 2g Fiber – 1g Sugar – 5g Protein

Polenta Fries with Chili-Lime Mayo

Serves: **4** ■ Temperature: **400°F** ■ Cooking Time: **28 minutes**

Easy

GF

Veg

2 teaspoons vegetable or olive oil

¼ teaspoon paprika

1 pound prepared polenta, cut into 3-inch x ½-inch sticks

salt and freshly ground black pepper

Chili-Lime Mayo

½ cup mayonnaise

1 teaspoon chili powder

¼ teaspoon ground cumin

juice of half a lime

1 teaspoon chopped fresh cilantro

salt and freshly ground black pepper

1. Pre-heat the air fryer to 400°F.

2. Combine the oil and paprika and then carefully toss the polenta sticks in the mixture.

3. Air-fry the polenta fries at 400°F for 15 minutes. Gently shake the basket to rotate the fries and continue to air-fry for another 13 minutes or until the fries have browned nicely. Season to taste with salt and freshly ground black pepper.

4. To make the chili-lime mayo, combine all the ingredients in a small bowl and stir well.

5. Serve the polenta fries warm with chili-lime mayo on the side for dipping.

Make Your Own

If you can't find prepared polenta in your grocery store, why not make your own? Bring 4 cups of water to a boil in a saucepan. Add 1 cup of dried polenta or cornmeal and whisk until the cornmeal is suspended in the water. Add 1 teaspoon of salt and let the cornmeal simmer for 15 to 20 minutes. Pour the finished polenta into an 8-inch square baking dish and let it cool completely (overnight in the refrigerator is best). Cut the firm polenta into sticks and then proceed with the recipe.

Per Serving
Polenta Fries 150 Calories – 2g Fat (0g Sat. Fat) – 0mg Cholesterol – 29g Carbohydrates – 2g Fiber – 0g Sugar – 4g Protein
Chili-Lime Mayo 190 Calories – 21g Fat (3g Sat. Fat) – 10mg Cholesterol – 1g Carbohydrates – 0g Fiber – 0g Sugar – 0g Protein

Cheeseburger Slider Pockets

Serves: **4 to 6** (makes 12 sliders) ■ Temperature: **350°F** ■ Cooking Time: **13 minutes per batch**

1 pound extra lean ground beef

2 teaspoons steak seasoning

2 tablespoons Worcestershire sauce

8 ounces Cheddar cheese

⅓ cup ketchup

¼ cup light mayonnaise

1 tablespoon pickle relish

1 pound frozen bread dough, defrosted

1 egg, beaten

sesame seeds

vegetable or olive oil, in a spray bottle

1. Combine the ground beef, steak seasoning and Worcestershire sauce in a large bowl. Divide the meat mixture into 12 equal portions. Cut the Cheddar cheese into twelve 2-inch squares, about ¼-inch thick. Stuff a square of cheese into the center of each portion of meat and shape into a 3-inch patty.

2. Make the slider sauce by combining the ketchup, mayonnaise, and relish in a small bowl. Set aside.

3. Cut the bread dough into twelve pieces. Shape each piece of dough into a ball and use a rolling pin to roll them out into 4-inch circles. Dollop ½ teaspoon of the slider sauce into the center of each dough circle. Place a beef patty on top of the sauce and wrap the dough around the patty, pinching the dough together to seal the pocket shut. Try not to stretch the dough too much when bringing the edges together. Brush both sides of the slider pocket with the beaten egg. Sprinkle sesame seeds on top of each pocket.

4. Preheat the air fryer to 350°F.

5. Spray or brush the bottom of the air fryer basket with oil. Air-fry the slider pockets four at a time. Transfer the slider pockets to the air fryer basket, seam side down and air-fry at 350°F for 10 minutes, until the dough is golden brown. Flip the slider pockets over and air-fry for another 3 minutes. When all the batches are done, pop all the sliders into the air fryer for a few minutes to re-heat and serve them hot out of the fryer.

Technique Tip

This recipe calls for extra lean ground beef because otherwise grease will leak out of the bread dough as it air-fries. You can substitute 80-20 (lean) ground beef if you prefer, but add a little water to the air fryer drawer to catch the grease and prevent it from smoking.

Per Slider 250 Calories – 11g Fat (5g Sat. Fat) – 50mg Cholesterol – 21g Carbohydrates – 1g Fiber – 4g Sugar – 15g Protein

Fantastic French Fries

No air fryer cookbook would be complete without some information on how to make one of everyone's favorite fried foods – French fries! French fries are an indulgence that so many of us love. The air fryer lets us love them without all the guilt.

■ **Pick the right potato.** Russet potatoes are my choice for French fries because their starch content gives the perfect tender center to the delicious brown salty exterior. Their low moisture content helps too. Waxy potatoes that are high in moisture tend to have hollow insides when made into French fries because the moisture evaporates.

■ **Cut them the right size.** The thinner you cut the potato, the crispier the French fry. If you like a French fry with a tender center, be sure to cut them big enough to achieve that goal – about ½-inch thick.

■ **To blanch or not to blanch?** In restaurants with a deep fryer, French fries are made crispy by double-frying them, sometimes at a low temperature first and then at a higher temperature. The first fry helps to cook the potatoes through and the second fry crisps them up. The quickest way to achieve the same results with an air fryer is to blanch the potato sticks first (drop them into boiling water for 4 minutes while the air fryer pre-heats) and then shock them by submerging them in ice water or running them under cold water. Dry them well and then spritz with oil and air-fry until they are brown and crispy and deliciously tender inside.

■ **Don't crowd them.** The air fryer cooks from the top down, so if you over-load the air fryer basket, the potato sticks on the bottom won't cook as well as those on the top. For crispier fries, don't overcrowd the basket, but cook in batches instead.

■ **Shake it up.** Here's where you get to have some fun! Shake the air fryer basket from time to time to rotate the fries. This helps them cook more evenly and lets you feel like the line cook you've always wanted to be!

■ **Top them your way.** French fries make the perfect base to top and season in any number of ways. Simple salt seasoning is a favorite, but you can be more adventurous with lemon zest, Parmesan cheese, parsley, chili flakes, or you can even make one of my favorite Canadian delicacies – poutine – by adding cheese curds and gravy!

Homemade French Fries

Serves: **2 to 3** ■ Temperature: **400°F** ■ Cooking Time: **25 minutes**

Easy
GF
Veg

2 to 3 russet potatoes, peeled and cut into ½-inch sticks

2 to 3 teaspoons olive or vegetable oil

salt

1. Bring a large pot of salted water to a boil while you peel and cut the potatoes. Blanch the potatoes in the boiling salted water for 4 minutes while you pre-heat the air fryer to 400°F. Strain the potatoes and rinse them with cold water. Dry them well with a clean kitchen towel.

2. Toss the dried potato sticks gently with the oil and place them in the air fryer basket. Air-fry at 400°F for 25 minutes, shaking the basket a few times while the fries cook to help them brown evenly. Season the fries with salt mid-way through cooking and serve them warm with tomato ketchup, Sriracha mayonnaise or a mix of lemon zest, Parmesan cheese and parsley. Yum!

Per Serving   130 Calories – 0g Fat (0g Sat. Fat) – 30g Carbohydrates – 2g Fiber – 4g Protein

Sweet Potato Fries
with Sweet and Spicy Dipping Sauce

Serves: **2 to 3** ■ Temperature: **200°F + 400°F** ■ Cooking Time: **20 minutes**

Easy

GF

Veg

1 large sweet potato (about 1 pound)

1 teaspoon vegetable or canola oil

salt

Sweet & Spicy Dipping Sauce

¼ cup light mayonnaise

1 tablespoon spicy brown mustard

1 tablespoon sweet Thai chili sauce

½ teaspoon sriracha sauce

1. Scrub the sweet potato well and then cut it into ¼-inch French fries. (A mandolin slicer can really help with this.)

2. Pre-heat the air fryer to 200°F.

3. Toss the sweet potato sticks with the oil and transfer them to the air fryer basket. Air-fry at 200°F for 10 minutes, shaking the basket several times during the cooking process for even cooking. Toss the fries with salt, increase the air fryer temperature to 400°F and air-fry for another 10 minutes, shaking the basket several times during the cooking process.

4. To make the dipping sauce, combine all the ingredients in a small bowl and stir until combined.

5. Serve the sweet potato fries warm with the dipping sauce on the side.

Note from Meredith

Sweet potato fries will never have the same texture as regular potato fries because of the moisture content inherent to each type of potato. However, the tender soft center of the sweet potato fry is often what most people like best about this snack-able vegetable. Getting the size of the fries consistent and no bigger than ½-inch thick is important to this recipe.

Per Serving
Sweet Potato Fries 130 Calories – 1g Fat (0g Sat. Fat) – 0mg Cholesterol – 28g Carbohydrates – 4g Fiber – 9g Sugar – 3g Protein
Sweet and Spicy Dipping Sauce 70 Calories – 4.5g Fat (0.5g Sat. Fat) – 5mg Cholesterol – 5g Carbohydrates – 0g Fiber – 3g Sugar – 0g Protein

Baked Ricotta with Lemon and Capers

Serves: **4 to 6** ■ Temperature: **380˚F** ■ Cooking Time: **8 to 10 minutes**

7-inch pie dish or cake pan

1½ cups whole milk ricotta cheese

zest of 1 lemon, plus more for garnish

1 teaspoon finely chopped fresh rosemary

pinch crushed red pepper flakes

2 tablespoons capers, rinsed

2 tablespoons extra-virgin olive oil

salt and freshly ground black pepper

1 tablespoon grated Parmesan cheese

1. Pre-heat the air fryer to 380°F.

2. Combine the ricotta cheese, lemon zest, rosemary, red pepper flakes, capers, olive oil, salt and pepper in a bowl and whisk together well. Transfer the cheese mixture to a 7-inch pie dish and place the pie dish in the air fryer basket. You can use an aluminum foil sling to help with this by taking a long piece of aluminum foil, folding it in half lengthwise twice until it is roughly 26 inches by 3 inches. Place this under the pie dish and hold the ends of the foil to move the pie dish in and out of the air fryer basket. Tuck the ends of the foil beside the pie dish while it cooks in the air fryer.

3. Air-fry the ricotta at 380°F for 8 to 10 minutes, or until the top is nicely browned in spots.

4. Remove the pie dish from the air fryer and immediately sprinkle the Parmesan cheese on top. Drizzle with a little olive oil and add some freshly ground black pepper and lemon zest as garnish. Serve warm with pita breads (see recipe on page 61) or crostini.

Easy

GF

Veg

Substitution Tip

You could add an egg to this dish and get a puffier result – just make sure you bake the mixture in a straight-sided pan. To make the recipe a little lighter, you could use part-skim ricotta cheese, but you'll miss the luxurious richness of the cheese. This is an appetizer or snack, so go for the whole milk version and share it with friends.

Per Serving 150 Calories – 13g Fat (6g Sat. Fat) – 30mg Cholesterol – 2g Carbohydrates – 0g Fiber – 0g Sugar – 7g Protein

Eggplant Parmesan Fries

Serves: **6** ■ Temperature: **400˚F** ■ Cooking Time: **9 minutes per batch**

Veg

GF*

½ cup all-purpose flour*

salt and freshly ground black pepper

2 eggs, beaten

1 cup seasoned breadcrumbs*

1 large eggplant

8 ounces mozzarella cheese
(aged or firm, not fresh)

olive oil, in a spray bottle

grated Parmesan cheese

1 (14-ounce) jar marinara sauce

*Make this recipe gluten free by using gluten-free flour and gluten-free breadcrumbs.

1. Create a dredging station with three shallow dishes. Place the flour in the first shallow dish and season well with salt and freshly ground black pepper. Put the eggs in the second shallow dish. Place the breadcrumbs in the third shallow dish.

2. Peel the eggplant and then slice it vertically into long ½-inch thick slices. Slice the mozzarella cheese into ½-inch thick slices and make a mozzarella sandwich, using the eggplant as the bread. Slice the eggplant-mozzarella sandwiches into rectangular strips about 1-inch by 3½-inches.

3. Coat the eggplant strips carefully, holding the sandwich together with your fingers. Dredge with flour first, then dip them into the eggs, and finally place them into the breadcrumbs. Pat the crumbs onto the eggplant strips and then coat them in the egg and breadcrumbs one more time, pressing gently with your hands so the crumbs stick evenly.

4. Pre-heat the air fryer to 400°F.

5. Spray the eggplant fries on all sides with olive oil, and transfer one layer at a time to the air-fryer basket. Air-fry in batches at 400°F for 9 minutes, turning and rotating halfway through the cooking time. Spray the eggplant strips with additional oil when you turn them over.

6. While the fries are cooking, gently warm the marinara sauce on the stovetop in a small saucepan.

7. Serve eggplant fries fresh out of the air fryer with a little Parmesan cheese grated on top and the warmed marinara sauce on the side.

Note from Meredith
This is like having a little eggplant Parmesan in the palm of your hand! If you want to be really fancy, you can square off your eggplant before you make the little sandwiches so that every "fry" is a perfect rectangle. Otherwise, you will have some fries with rounded edges, but I promise you the round ones will taste just as good!

Per Serving 210 Calories – 11g Fat (6g Sat. Fat) – 45mg Cholesterol – 16g Carbohydrates – 4g Fiber – 7g Sugar – 12g Protein

Spicy Chicken and Pepper Jack Cheese Bites

Serves: **8** ■ Temperature: **400°F** ■ Cooking Time: **8 minutes per batch**

8 ounces cream cheese, softened

2 cups grated pepper jack cheese

1 Jalapeño pepper, diced

2 scallions, minced

1 teaspoon paprika

2 teaspoons salt, divided

3 cups shredded cooked chicken

¼ cup all-purpose flour*

2 eggs, lightly beaten

1 cup panko breadcrumbs*

olive oil, in a spray bottle

salsa

*Make this recipe gluten free by using gluten-free flour and gluten-free breadcrumbs.

1. Beat the cream cheese in a bowl until it is smooth and easy to stir. Add the pepper jack cheese, Jalapeño pepper, scallions, paprika and 1 teaspoon of salt. Fold in the shredded cooked chicken and combine well. Roll this mixture into 1-inch balls.

2. Set up a dredging station with three shallow dishes. Place the flour into one shallow dish. Place the eggs into a second shallow dish. Finally, combine the panko breadcrumbs and remaining teaspoon of salt in a third dish.

3. Coat the chicken cheese balls by rolling each ball in the flour first, then dip them into the eggs and finally roll them in the panko breadcrumbs to coat all sides. Refrigerate for at least 30 minutes.

4. Preheat the air fryer to 400°F.

5. Spray the chicken cheese balls with oil and air-fry in batches for 8 minutes. Shake the basket a few times throughout the cooking process to help the balls brown evenly.

6. Serve hot with salsa on the side.

GF*

Make it Ahead

These chicken cheese balls also freeze really well. Freeze them on a cookie sheet before you air-fry them in step 4. When you're ready to cook them, let them sit on the countertop for 30 minutes before proceeding with the recipe.

Per Serving 310 Calories – 20g Fat (11g Sat. Fat) – 115mg Cholesterol – 6g Carbohydrates – 0g Fiber – 1g Sugar – 25g Protein

Sweet and Salty Snack Mix

Makes: **about 10 cups** ■ Temperature: **370°F** ■ Cooking Time: **10 to 12 minutes per batch**

½ cup honey

3 tablespoons butter, melted

1 teaspoon salt

2 cups sesame sticks

1 cup pepitas (pumpkin seeds)

2 cups granola

1 cup cashews

2 cups crispy corn puff cereal
(Kix® or Corn Pops®)

2 cups mini pretzel crisps

1 cup dried cherries

1. Combine the honey, butter and salt in a small bowl or measuring cup and stir until combined.

2. Combine the sesame sticks, pepitas, granola, cashews, corn puff cereal and pretzel crisps in a large bowl. Pour the honey mixture over the top and toss to combine.

3. Preheat air fryer to 370°F.

4. Air-fry the snack mix in two batches. Place half the mixture in the air fryer basket and air-fry for 10 to 12 minutes, or until the snack mix is lightly toasted. Toss the basket several times throughout the process so that the mix cooks evenly and doesn't get too dark on top.

5. Transfer the snack mix to a cookie sheet and let it cool completely. Mix in the dried cherries and store the mix in an airtight container for up to a week or two.

Easy

Veg

Note from Meredith

This is a really nice and easy gift to make for friends and family at the holidays or any time of year. Transfer the snack mix to cute bags or jars and dress them up with a ribbon. Homemade gifts are always the best gifts.

Per ½ cup of mix 270 Calories – 12g Fat (3g Sat. Fat) – 5mg Cholesterol – 35g Carbohydrates – 3g Fiber – 15g Sugar – 6g Protein

Fried Cheese Ravioli with Marinara Sauce

Serves: **4 to 6** ■ Temperature: **380°F** ■ Cooking Time: **7 minutes per batch**

1 pound cheese ravioli, fresh or frozen

2 eggs, lightly beaten

1 cup plain breadcrumbs

½ teaspoon paprika

½ teaspoon dried oregano

½ teaspoon salt

grated Parmesan cheese

chopped fresh parsley

1 to 2 cups marinara sauce
(jarred or homemade)

1. Bring a stockpot of salted water to a boil. Boil the ravioli according to the package directions and then drain. Let the cooked ravioli cool to a temperature where you can comfortably handle them.

2. While the pasta is cooking, set up a dredging station with two shallow dishes. Place the eggs into one dish. Combine the breadcrumbs, paprika, dried oregano and salt in the other dish.

3. Pre-heat the air fryer to 380°F.

4. Working with one at a time, dip the cooked ravioli into the egg, coating all sides. Then press the ravioli into the breadcrumbs, making sure that all sides are covered. Transfer the ravioli to the air fryer basket, cooking in batches, one layer at a time. Air-fry at 380°F for 7 minutes.

5. While the ravioli is air-frying, bring the marinara sauce to a simmer on the stovetop. Transfer to a small bowl.

6. Sprinkle a little Parmesan cheese and chopped parsley on top of the fried ravioli and serve warm with the marinara sauce on the side for dipping.

Preparation Tip

You can actually make fried ravioli without boiling the ravioli first if you're in a real hurry. They won't be as tender on the inside, but they will be super crispy. Cook from frozen and use the same cooking temperature, but add a minute to the cooking time.

Per Serving 60 Calories – 1g Fat (0g Sat. Fat) – 15mg Cholesterol – 9g Carbohydrates – 1g Fiber – 3g Sugar – 2g Protein

Veggie Chips

Serves: **varies** ■ Temperature: **400°F** ■ Cooking Time: **varies by vegetable**

Easy

GF

Veg

sweet potato

large parsnip

large carrot

turnip

large beet

vegetable or canola oil, in a spray bottle

salt

1. You can do a medley of vegetable chips, or just select from the vegetables listed. Whatever you choose to do, scrub the vegetables well and then slice them paper-thin using a mandolin (about 1/16-inch thick).

2. Pre-heat the air fryer to 400°F.

3. Air-fry the chips in batches, one type of vegetable at a time. Spray the chips lightly with oil and transfer them to the air fryer basket. The key is to NOT over-load the basket. You can overlap the chips a little, but don't pile them on top of each other. Doing so will make it much harder to get evenly browned and crispy chips. Air-fry at 400°F for the time indicated below, shaking the basket several times during the cooking process for even cooking.

   Sweet Potato – 8 to 9 minutes
   Parsnips – 5 minutes
   Carrot – 7 minutes
   Turnips – 8 minutes
   Beets – 9 minutes

Season the chips with salt during the last couple of minutes of air-frying. Check the chips as they cook until they are done to your liking. Some will start to brown sooner than others.

4. You can enjoy the chips warm out of the air fryer or cool them to room temperature for crispier chips. These are best enjoyed the day they are made, however.

Technique Tip
The secret to making these chips is to make them in batches and not too many at one time. If you give the chips room for the air to circulate easily, they crisp up with dark brown edges and have a delicious crunchy texture. Spraying with a little oil partway through the cooking process will also help crisp up the chips.

Varies by vegetable The following includes 1 of each vegetable and 10 servings per recipe. 35 Calories – 1g Fat (0g Sat. Fat) – 0mg Cholesterol – 7g Carbohydrates – 2g Fiber – 2g Sugar – 1g Protein

Dill Fried Pickles with Light Ranch Dip

Serves: **4** ■ Temperature: **400°F** ■ Cooking Time: **8 minutes per batch**

4 to 6 large dill pickles, sliced in half or quartered lengthwise

½ cup all-purpose flour*

2 eggs, lightly beaten

1 cup plain breadcrumbs*

1 teaspoon salt

⅛ teaspoon cayenne pepper

2 tablespoons fresh dill leaves, dried well

vegetable oil, in a spray bottle

Light Ranch Dip

¼ cup reduced-fat mayonnaise

¼ cup buttermilk

¼ cup non-fat Greek yogurt

1 tablespoon chopped fresh chives

1 tablespoon chopped fresh parsley

1 tablespoon lemon juice

salt and freshly ground black pepper

*Make this recipe gluten free by using gluten-free flour and gluten-free breadcrumbs.

1. Dry the dill pickle spears very well with a clean kitchen towel.

2. Set up a dredging station using three shallow dishes. Place the flour in the first shallow dish. Place the eggs into the second dish. Combine the breadcrumbs, salt, cayenne and fresh dill in a food processor and process until everything is combined and the crumbs are very fine. Place the crumb mixture in the third dish.

3. Pre-heat the air fryer to 400°F.

4. Coat the pickles by dredging them first in the flour, then the egg, and then the breadcrumbs, pressing the crumbs on gently with your hands. Set the coated pickles on a tray and spray them on all sides with vegetable oil.

5. Air-fry one layer of pickles at a time at 400°F for 8 minutes, turning them over halfway through the cooking process and spraying lightly again if necessary. The crumbs should be nicely browned on all sides.

6. While the pickles are air-frying, make the light ranch dip by mixing everything together in a bowl. Serve the pickles warm with the dip on the side.

Easy

GF*

Veg

Note from Meredith

I call these "Dill Fried Pickles" rather than "Fried Dill Pickles" because the added boost of fresh dill in the breadcrumbs gives it that extra burst of flavor. The dill will even turn the breadcrumbs a little green, which makes for an interesting appearance too. Maybe the perfect St. Patrick's Day snack?

Per Serving
Dill Fried Pickles 90 Calories – 1.5g Fat (0g Sat. Fat) – 25mg Cholesterol – 16g Carbohydrates – 2g Fiber – 2g Sugar – 3g Protein
Light Ranch Dip 80 Calories – 6g Fat (1g Sat. Fat) – 10mg Cholesterol – 4g Carbohydrates – 0g Fiber – 3g Sugar – 3g Protein

Shrimp Toasts

Serves: **4 to 6** ■ Temperature: **400°F** ■ Cooking Time: **6 to 8 minutes per batch**

½ pound raw shrimp,
peeled and de-veined

1 egg (or 2 egg whites)

2 scallions, plus more for garnish

2 teaspoons grated fresh ginger

1 teaspoon soy sauce

½ teaspoon toasted sesame oil

2 tablespoons chopped fresh cilantro
or parsley

1 to 2 teaspoons sriracha sauce

6 slices thinly-sliced white sandwich bread
(Pepperidge Farm®)

½ cup sesame seeds

Thai chili sauce

Easy

1. Combine the shrimp, egg, scallions, fresh ginger, soy sauce, sesame oil, cilantro (or parsley) and sriracha sauce in a food processor and process into a chunky paste, scraping down the sides of the food processor bowl as necessary.

2. Cut the crusts off the sandwich bread and generously spread the shrimp paste onto each slice of bread. Place the sesame seeds on a plate and invert each shrimp toast into the sesame seeds to coat, pressing down gently. Cut each slice of bread into 4 triangles.

3. Pre-heat the air fryer to 400°F.

4. Transfer one layer of shrimp toast triangles to the air fryer and air-fry at 400°F for 6 to 8 minutes, or until the sesame seeds are toasted on top.

5. Serve warm with a little Thai chili sauce and some sliced scallions as garnish.

Shopping Tip

Don't spend your money on jumbo shrimp for this recipe – everything gets processed in a food processor anyway, so the size of your shrimp doesn't matter. Getting previously peeled and deveined shrimp will save you time, however.

Per Serving 180 Calories – 7g Fat (1g Sat. Fat) – 80mg Cholesterol – 14g Carbohydrates – 2g Fiber – 4g Sugar – 13g Protein

Avocado Fries with Quick Salsa Fresca

Serves: **4 to 6** ■ Temperature: **400˚F** ■ Cooking Time: **6 minutes per batch**

Easy
GF*
Veg

½ cup flour*

2 teaspoons salt

2 eggs, lightly beaten

1 cup panko breadcrumbs*

⅛ teaspoon cayenne pepper

¼ teaspoon smoked paprika (optional)

2 large avocados, just ripe

vegetable oil, in a spray bottle

Quick Salsa Fresca

1 cup cherry tomatoes

1 tablespoon-sized chunk of shallot or red onion

2 teaspoons fresh lime juice

1 teaspoon chopped fresh cilantro or parsley

salt and freshly ground black pepper

*Make this recipe gluten free by using gluten-free flour and gluten-free breadcrumbs.

1. Set up a dredging station with three shallow dishes. Place the flour and salt in the first shallow dish. Place the eggs into the second dish. Combine the breadcrumbs, cayenne pepper and paprika (if using) in the third dish.

2. Pre-heat the air fryer to 400°F.

3. Cut the avocado in half around the pit and separate the two sides. Slice the avocados into long strips while still in their skin. Run a spoon around the slices, separating them from the avocado skin. Try to keep the slices whole, but don't worry if they break – you can still coat and air-fry the pieces.

4. Coat the avocado slices by dredging them first in the flour, then the egg and then the breadcrumbs, pressing the crumbs on gently with your hands. Set the coated avocado fries on a tray and spray them on all sides with vegetable oil.

5. Air-fry the avocado fries, one layer at a time, at 400°F for 6 minutes, turning them over halfway through the cooking time and spraying lightly again if necessary. When the fries are nicely browned on all sides, season with salt and remove.

6. While the avocado fries are air-frying, make the salsa fresca by combining everything in a food processor. Pulse several times until the salsa is a chunky purée. Serve the fries warm with the salsa on the side for dipping.

Shopping Tip

Picking the right avocados is key to this recipe. When selecting avocados in the grocery store, give them a gentle squeeze. You want an avocado that yields ever so slightly to your pressure – just ripe or almost ripe is better than too ripe. If it's too ripe, the avocado will be very hard to coat and air-fry. One fail-safe way to go about this is to get avocados that are a little under-ripe and use them once they ripen perfectly on your kitchen counter, in a day or so.

Per Serving
Avocado Fries   130 Calories – 10g Fat (1.5g Sat. Fat) – 5mg Cholesterol – 10g Carbohydrates – 5g Fiber – 1g Sugar – 2g Protein
Quick Salsa Fresca   10 Calories – 0g Fat (0g Sat. Fat) – 0mg Cholesterol – 2g Carbohydrates – 1g Fiber – 1g Sugar – 0g Protein

Fried Brie with Cherry Tomatoes

Serves: **8** ■ Temperature: **350˚F** ■ Cooking Time: **15 minutes (+ time to make crostini)**

1 baguette*

2 pints red and yellow cherry tomatoes

1 tablespoon olive oil

salt and freshly ground black pepper

1 teaspoon balsamic vinegar

1 tablespoon chopped fresh parsley

1 (8-ounce) wheel of Brie cheese

olive oil

½ teaspoon Italian seasoning (optional)

1 tablespoon chopped fresh basil

*Make this recipe gluten free by using gluten-free crostini.

Easy

GF*

Veg

1. Pre-heat the air fryer to 350°F.

2. Start by making the crostini. Slice the baguette diagonally into ½-inch slices and brush the slices with olive oil on both sides. Air-fry the baguette slices at 350°F in batches for 6 minutes or until lightly browned on all sides. Set the bread aside on your serving platter.

3. Toss the cherry tomatoes in a bowl with the olive oil, salt and pepper. Air-fry the cherry tomatoes for 3 to 5 minutes, shaking the basket a few times during the cooking process. The tomatoes should be soft and some of them will burst open. Toss the warm tomatoes with the balsamic vinegar and fresh parsley and set aside.

4. Cut a circle of parchment paper the same size as your wheel of Brie cheese. Brush both sides of the Brie wheel with olive oil and sprinkle with Italian seasoning, if using. Place the circle of parchment paper on one side of the Brie and transfer the Brie to the air fryer basket, parchment side down. Air-fry at 350°F for 8 to 10 minutes, or until the Brie is slightly puffed and soft to the touch.

5. Watch carefully and remove the Brie before the rind cracks and the cheese starts to leak out. Transfer the wheel to your serving platter and top with the roasted tomatoes. Sprinkle with basil and serve with the toasted bread slices.

Serving Suggestion

You don't have to make your own crostini for this delicious appetizer (although it's so very easy). You can serve the brie and tomatoes with crackers (gluten-free if you like), fresh bread or even vegetables like cucumber or endive spears.

Per Serving 160 Calories – 10g Fat (5g Sat. Fat) – 30mg Cholesterol – 10g Carbohydrates – 1g Fiber – 2g Sugar – 7g Protein

Mozzarella en Carrozza
with Puttanesca Sauce

Serves: **6 to 8** ■ Temperature: **390°F** ■ Cooking Time: **8 minutes per batch**

Puttanesca Sauce

2 teaspoons olive oil

1 anchovy, chopped (optional)

2 cloves garlic, minced

1 (14-ounce) can petite diced tomatoes

½ cup chicken stock or water

⅓ cup Kalamata olives, chopped

2 tablespoons capers

½ teaspoon dried oregano

¼ teaspoon crushed red pepper flakes

salt and freshly ground black pepper

1 tablespoon fresh parsley, chopped

8 slices of thinly sliced white bread
(Pepperidge Farm®)

8 ounces mozzarella cheese, cut into
¼-inch slices

½ cup all-purpose flour

3 eggs, beaten

1½ cups seasoned panko breadcrumbs

½ teaspoon garlic powder

½ teaspoon salt

freshly ground black pepper

olive oil, in a spray bottle

1. Start by making the puttanesca sauce. Heat the olive oil in a medium saucepan on the stovetop. Add the anchovies (if using, and I really think you should!) and garlic and sauté for 3 minutes, or until the anchovies have "melted" into the oil. Add the tomatoes, chicken stock, olives, capers, oregano and crushed red pepper flakes and simmer the sauce for 20 minutes. Season with salt and freshly ground black pepper and stir in the fresh parsley.

2. Cut the crusts off the slices of bread. Place four slices of the bread on a cutting board. Divide the cheese between the four slices of bread. Top the cheese with the remaining four slices of bread to make little sandwiches and cut each sandwich into 4 triangles.

3. Set up a dredging station using three shallow dishes. Place the flour in the first shallow dish, the eggs in the second dish and in the third dish, combine the panko breadcrumbs, garlic powder, salt and black pepper. Dredge each little triangle in the flour first (you might think this is redundant, but it helps to get the coating to adhere to the edges of the sandwiches) and then dip them into the egg, making sure both the sides and the edges are coated. Let the excess egg drip off and then press the triangles into the breadcrumb mixture, pressing the crumbs on with your hands so they adhere. Place the coated triangles in the freezer for 2 hours, until the cheese is frozen.

4. Pre-heat the air fryer to 390°F. Spray all sides of the mozzarella triangles with oil and transfer a single layer of triangles to the air fryer basket. Air-fry in batches at 390°F for 5 minutes. Turn the triangles over and air-fry for an additional 3 minutes.

5. Serve mozzarella triangles immediately with the warm puttanesca sauce.

Make it Ahead
You'll be happy to hear that you can make these ahead of time! Once the mozzarella is frozen after step 3, transfer the frozen triangles to freezer bags and then air-fry them from frozen any time you fancy a delicious snack or for your next party.

Per Serving
Mozzarella en Carrozza 160 Calories – 8g Fat (4g Sat. Fat) – 50mg Cholesterol –
13g Carbohydrates – 1g Fiber – 2g Sugar – 9g Protein
Puttanesca Sauce 60 Calories – 4g Fat (0.5g Sat. Fat) – 0mg Cholesterol –
4g Carbohydrates – 1g Fiber – 1g Sugar – 1g Protein

Breads &
Breakfast

Garlic Parmesan Bread Ring

Serves: **6 to 8** ■ Temperature: **340°F** ■ Cooking Time: **30 minutes**

½ cup unsalted butter, melted

¼ teaspoon salt
(omit if using salted butter)

¾ cup grated Parmesan cheese

3 to 4 cloves garlic, minced

1 tablespoon chopped fresh parsley

1 pound frozen bread dough, defrosted

olive oil

1 egg, beaten

1. Combine the melted butter, salt, Parmesan cheese, garlic and chopped parsley in a small bowl.

2. Roll the dough out into a rectangle that measures 8 inches by 17 inches. Spread the butter mixture over the dough, leaving a half-inch border un-buttered along one of the long edges. Roll the dough from one long edge to the other, ending with the un-buttered border. Pinch the seam shut tightly. Shape the log into a circle sealing the ends together by pushing one end into the other and stretching the dough around it.

3. Cut out a circle of aluminum foil that is the same size as the air fryer basket. Brush the foil circle with oil and place an oven safe ramekin or glass in the center. Transfer the dough ring to the aluminum foil circle, around the ramekin. This will help you make sure the dough will fit in the basket and maintain its ring shape. Use kitchen shears to cut 8 slits around the outer edge of the dough ring halfway to the center. Brush the dough ring with egg wash.

4. Pre-heat the air fryer to 400°F for 4 minutes. When it has pre-heated, brush the sides of the basket with oil and transfer the dough ring, foil circle and ramekin into the basket. Slide the drawer back into the air fryer, but do not turn the air fryer on. Let the dough rise inside the warm air fryer for 30 minutes.

5. After the bread has proofed in the air fryer for 30 minutes, set the temperature to 340°F and air-fry the bread ring for 15 minutes. Flip the bread over by inverting it onto a plate or cutting board and sliding it back into the air fryer basket. Air-fry for another 15 minutes. Let the bread cool for a few minutes before slicing the bread ring in between the slits and serving warm.

Technique Tip

This recipe uses a handy technique for dough – using a pre-heated, but turned off air fryer as a proof box. It's always best to let your dough rise in a warm place and the air fryer is a perfect place for this.

Per Serving 300 Calories - 17g Fat (9g Sat. Fat) - 55mg Cholesterol - 28g Carbohydrates - 1g Fiber - 2g Sugar - 8g Protein

Mini Pita Breads

Makes: **8 mini pitas** ■ Temperature: **400°F** ■ Cooking Time: **6 minutes per bread**

Veg

2 teaspoons active dry yeast

1 tablespoon sugar

1¼ to 1½ cups warm water (90° - 110°F)

3¼ cups all-purpose flour

2 teaspoons salt

1 tablespoon olive oil, plus more for brushing

kosher salt (optional)

Note from Meredith
Of course, you'll want to serve your pita breads with a little hummus...

1. Dissolve the yeast, sugar and water in the bowl of a stand mixer. Let the mixture sit for 5 minutes to make sure the yeast is active – it should foam a little. (If there's no foaming, discard and start again with new yeast.) Combine the flour and salt in a bowl, and add it to the water, along with the olive oil. Mix with the dough hook until combined. Add a little more flour if needed to get the dough to pull away from the sides of the mixing bowl, or add a little more water if the dough seems too dry.

2. Knead the dough until it is smooth and elastic (about 8 minutes in the mixer or 15 minutes by hand). Transfer the dough to a lightly oiled bowl, cover and let it rise in a warm place until doubled in bulk. (See page 61 for a tip on this.)

3. Divide the dough into 8 portions and roll each portion into a circle about 4-inches in diameter. Don't roll the balls too thin, or you won't get the pocket inside the pita.

4. Pre-heat the air fryer to 400°F.

5. Brush both sides of the dough with olive oil, and sprinkle with kosher salt if desired. Air-fry one at a time at 400°F for 6 minutes, flipping it over when there are two minutes left in the cooking time.

Hummus

2 (15-ounce) cans chickpeas, drained and rinsed well (about 3 cups)

2 to 4 cloves garlic

1 cup tahini (sesame paste)

3 to 4 tablespoons fresh lemon juice (about 1 lemon)

1 to 1½ teaspoons salt

2 tablespoons olive oil

6 to 8 tablespoons cold water

extra virgin olive oil, chopped fresh parsley and sweet paprika (for serving)

1. Rinse the chickpeas well with warm water and set aside. Most canned chickpeas are already salted, so be aware of this as you add salt in the next step.

2. Start with the food processor running and drop in the garlic cloves. Add the chickpeas and process the chickpeas until they form a paste. With the food processor still running, drizzle in the tahini, lemon juice and salt and continue to process. Drizzle in the olive oil and then add as much cold water as you need to get the texture you want, processing for 5 minutes until smooth.

3. Taste the hummus and season again to taste, adding more lemon juice or salt as needed. Serves 8.

Per Serving
Per pita bread 220 Calories - 3g Fat (0g Sat. Fat) - 0mg Cholesterol - 41g Carbohydrates - 2g Fiber - 2g Sugar - 6g Protein
Hummus 290 Calories - 20g Fat (2.5g Sat. Fat) - 0mg Cholesterol - 23g Carbohydrates - 7g Fiber - 4g Sugar - 10g Protein

Making Dough

The most delicious doughs are either baked or fried – fried donuts, baked pizza, fried beignets, baked bread rolls... I could go on. An air fryer uses convection heat to replicate fried results, so it's no surprise that it is a perfect appliance to turn dough into something delectable. With a few helpful hints, you can use your air fryer for successful breads, pizzas and pastries.

Use your air fryer for proofing dough. One of my favorite discoveries in working with the air fryer is using it as a proofing box. Proofing is an important step in making yeast dough – allowing the dough to rest and rise in a warm moist environment. Common household tricks for creating such an environment include putting a sheet pan of boiling water into your turned off oven, or boiling a bowl of water in a microwave, or simply just putting the dough in a part of your house that is generally warmer than the rest of the house. The air fryer can work the same way. Pre-heat the air fryer for several minutes and then put the dough (in an oiled bowl) in the turned off fryer. If you want a really moist environment for the dough, pre-heat the air fryer with a cup of water in the bottom drawer.

Oil the dough. When you're ready to air-fry your dough, make sure you oil the dough first. While many air fryers have a non-stick basket, dough can be a little sticky, so it is a good assurance to oil the dough on both sides lightly before placing it into the pre-heated air fryer.

Give it a flip. Air fryers cook from the top down, so in order to brown and cook both sides, give the dough a flip halfway through the cooking time.

Wash up first! To give your dough a nice color or a nice shine, brush it with a little egg wash before you air-fry it. A wash is simply an egg, lightly beaten, often with something added to it, like water, cream, salt or milk. Different ingredients in the wash have different affects on dough. Protein will enhance the browning of the dough. Fat will help give the dough a shine. So, egg yolk and cream will increase the shine, while egg white and milk will help it brown. Water and salt are sometimes added to thin the egg wash, making it easier to spread. Water just dilutes the wash, while salt is added to break down the egg whites.

Pizza Dough

Makes 3 (6- to 8-ounce) dough balls

4 cups bread flour, pizza ("00") flour or all-purpose flour

1 teaspoon active dry yeast

2 teaspoons sugar

2 teaspoons salt

1½ cups water

1 tablespoon olive oil

1. Combine the flour, yeast, sugar and salt in the bowl of a stand mixer. Add the olive oil to the flour mixture and start to mix using the dough hook attachment. As you're mixing, add 1¼ cups of the water, mixing until the dough comes together. Continue to knead the dough with the dough hook for another 10 minutes, adding enough water to the dough to get it to the right consistency.

2. Transfer the dough to a floured counter and divide it into 3 equal portions. Roll each portion into a ball. Lightly coat each dough ball with oil and transfer to the refrigerator, covered with plastic wrap. You can place them all on a baking sheet, or place each dough ball into its own oiled zipper sealable plastic bag or container. (You can freeze the dough balls at this stage, removing as much air as possible from the oiled bag.) Keep in the refrigerator for at least one day, or as long as five days.

3. When you're ready to use the dough, remove your dough from the refrigerator at least 1 hour prior to baking and let it sit on the counter, covered gently with plastic wrap.

Spinach and Artichoke White Pizza

Serves: 2   ■   Temperature: 390°F + 350°F   ■   Cooking Time: 10 + 8 minutes

olive oil

3 cups fresh spinach

2 cloves garlic, minced, divided

1 (6- to 8-ounce) pizza dough ball*

½ cup grated mozzarella cheese

¼ cup grated Fontina cheese

¼ cup artichoke hearts, coarsely chopped

2 tablespoons grated Parmesan cheese

¼ teaspoon dried oregano

salt and freshly ground black pepper

*You can make this recipe gluten free by using a gluten-free pizza dough.

1. Heat the oil in a medium sauté pan on the stovetop. Add the spinach and half the minced garlic to the pan and sauté for a few minutes, until the spinach has wilted. Remove the sautéed spinach from the pan and set it aside.

2. Pre-heat the air fryer to 390°F.

3. Cut out a piece of aluminum foil the same size as the bottom of the air fryer basket. Brush the foil circle with olive oil. Shape the dough into a circle and place it on top of the foil. Dock the dough by piercing it several times with a fork. Brush the dough lightly with olive oil and transfer it into the air fryer basket with the foil on the bottom.

4. Air-fry the plain pizza dough for 6 minutes. Turn the dough over, remove the aluminum foil and brush again with olive oil. Air-fry for an additional 4 minutes.

5. Sprinkle the mozzarella and Fontina cheeses over the dough. Top with the spinach and artichoke hearts. Sprinkle the Parmesan cheese and dried oregano on top and drizzle with olive oil. Lower the temperature of the air fryer to 350°F and cook for 8 minutes, until the cheese has melted and is lightly browned. Season to taste with salt and freshly ground black pepper.

Veg
GF*

Make it Yourself
You can use your favorite store-bought pizza dough for this recipe, or you can try the recipe listed on page 62. That recipe will make three (6- to 8-ounce) dough balls.

Per Serving 500 Calories – 16g Fat (7g Sat. Fat) – 35mg Cholesterol - 62g Carbohydrates – 3g Fiber - 2g Sugar - 25g Protein

Sweet-Hot Pepperoni Pizza

Serves: 2 ■ Temperature: 390˚F + 350˚F ■ Cooking Time: 10 + 8 minutes

GF*

1 (6- to 8-ounce) pizza dough ball*

olive oil

½ cup pizza sauce

¾ cup grated mozzarella cheese

½ cup thick sliced pepperoni

⅓ cup sliced pickled hot banana peppers

¼ teaspoon dried oregano

2 teaspoons honey

*You can make this recipe gluten free by using a gluten-free pizza dough.

1. Pre-heat the air fryer to 390°F.

2. Cut out a piece of aluminum foil the same size as the bottom of the air fryer basket. Brush the foil circle with olive oil. Shape the dough into a circle and place it on top of the foil. Dock the dough by piercing it several times with a fork. Brush the dough lightly with olive oil and transfer it into the air fryer basket with the foil on the bottom.

3. Air-fry the plain pizza dough for 6 minutes. Turn the dough over, remove the aluminum foil and brush again with olive oil. Air-fry for an additional 4 minutes.

4. Spread the pizza sauce on top of the dough and sprinkle the mozzarella cheese over the sauce. Top with the pepperoni, pepper slices and dried oregano. Lower the temperature of the air fryer to 350°F and cook for 8 minutes, until the cheese has melted and lightly browned. Transfer the pizza to a cutting board and drizzle with the honey. Slice and serve.

Note from Meredith

I love the combination of spicy and sweet flavors and this pizza is a great example. Of course, you can omit the honey if it's not your 'thing'... but I'd give it a try at least once. 😊

Per Serving 980 Calories – 59g Fat (24g Sat. Fat) – 130mg Cholesterol – 67g Carbohydrates – 2g Fiber – 8g Sugar – 38g Protein

Cheesy Olive and Roasted Pepper Bread

Serves: **8** ■ Temperature: **370°F + 350°F** ■ Cooking Time: **7 minutes per batch**

Veg

7-inch round bread boule

olive oil

½ cup mayonnaise

2 tablespoons butter, melted

1 cup grated mozzarella
or Fontina cheese

¼ cup grated Parmesan cheese

½ teaspoon dried oregano

½ cup black olives, sliced

½ cup green olives, sliced

½ cup coarsely chopped roasted
red peppers

2 tablespoons minced red onion

freshly ground black pepper

1. Pre-heat the air fryer to 370°F.

2. Cut the bread boule in half horizontally. If your bread boule has a rounded top, trim the top of the boule so that the top half will lie flat with the cut side facing up. Lightly brush both sides of the boule halves with olive oil.

3. Place one half of the boule into the air fryer basket with the center cut side facing down. Air-fry at 370°F for 2 minutes to lightly toast the bread. Repeat with the other half of the bread boule.

4. Combine the mayonnaise, butter, mozzarella cheese, Parmesan cheese and dried oregano in a small bowl. Fold in the black and green olives, roasted red peppers and red onion and season with freshly ground black pepper. Spread the cheese mixture over the untoasted side of the bread, covering the entire surface.

5. Air-fry at 350°F for 5 minutes until the cheese is melted and browned. Repeat with the other half. Cut into slices and serve warm.

Substitution Tip
If you can't find a round bread boule, you can use ciabatta rolls for this recipe. Simply cut them in half and make smaller versions of the above.

Per Serving 340 Calories – 22g Fat (8g Sat. Fat) – 30mg Cholesterol – 12g Carbohydrates – 0g Fiber – 1g Sugar – 10g Protein

French Toast and Turkey Sausage Roll-Ups

Serves: **3**   ▪   Temperature: **380°F + 370°F**   ▪   Cooking Time: **10 + 14 minutes**

Easy

GF*

6 links turkey sausage

6 slices of white bread, crusts removed*

2 eggs

½ cup milk

½ teaspoon ground cinnamon

½ teaspoon vanilla extract

1 tablespoon butter, melted

powdered sugar (optional)

maple syrup

*You can make this recipe gluten free by using gluten-free bread.

1. Pre-heat the air fryer to 380°F and pour a little water into the bottom of the air fryer drawer. (This will help prevent the grease that drips into the bottom drawer from burning and smoking.)

2. Air-fry the sausage links at 380°F for 8 to 10 minutes, turning them a couple of times during the cooking process. (If you have pre-cooked sausage links, omit this step.)

3. Roll each sausage link in a piece of bread, pressing the finished seam tightly to seal shut.

4. Pre-heat the air fryer to 370°F.

5. Combine the eggs, milk, cinnamon, and vanilla in a shallow dish. Dip the sausage rolls in the egg mixture and let them soak in the egg for 30 seconds. Spray or brush the bottom of the air fryer basket with oil and transfer the sausage rolls to the basket, seam side down.

6. Air-fry the rolls at 370°F for 9 minutes. Brush melted butter over the bread, flip the rolls over and air-fry for an additional 5 minutes. Remove the French toast roll-ups from the basket and dust with powdered sugar, if using. Serve with maple syrup and enjoy.

Substitution Tip

You can substitute any type of sausage that you like for this recipe. Breakfast pork sausage would be delicious, but you'll spend a few more calories. This recipe calls for the classic white bread slices because they have the most neutral flavor and also because they are soft enough to easily seal the seam. You could, of course, substitute wheat or whole grain bread instead if that's what you prefer.

Per Serving   410 Calories – 15g Fat (5g Sat. Fat) – 135mg Cholesterol – 59g Carbohydrates – 0g Fiber – 56g Sugar – 11g Protein

Hush Puffins

Makes: **20 to 22** ■ Temperature: **360˚F** ■ Cooking Time: **8 minutes per batch**

Veg

1 cup buttermilk

¼ cup butter, melted

2 eggs

1½ cups all-purpose flour

1½ cups cornmeal

⅓ cup sugar

1 teaspoon baking soda

1 teaspoon salt

4 scallions, minced

vegetable oil

1. Combine the buttermilk, butter and eggs in a large mixing bowl. In a second bowl combine the flour, cornmeal, sugar, baking soda and salt. Add the dry ingredients to the wet ingredients, stirring just to combine. Stir in the minced scallions and refrigerate the batter for 30 minutes.

2. Shape the batter into 2-inch balls. Brush or spray the balls with oil.

3. Pre-heat the air fryer to 360°F.

4. Air-fry the hush puffins in two batches at 360°F for 8 minutes, turning them over after 6 minutes of the cooking process.

5. Serve warm with butter.

Note from Meredith

These little delights are half hushpuppy and half corn muffin... hence Hush Puffins! Enjoy!

Per 3 puffins 290 Calories – 10g Fat (5g Sat. Fat) – 70mg Cholesterol – 41g Carbohydrates – 3g Fiber – 2g Sugar – 5g Protein

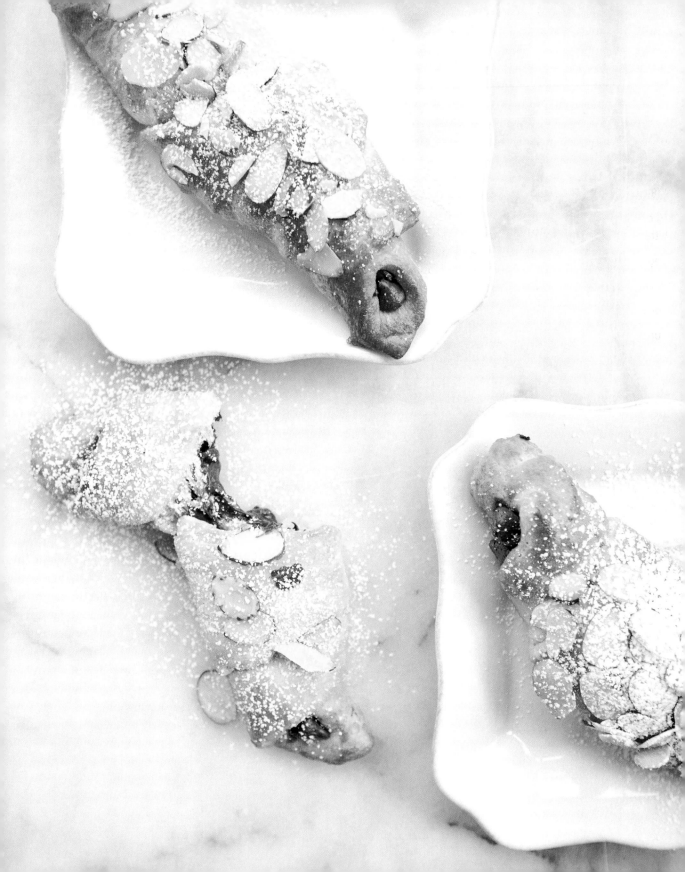

Chocolate Almond Crescent Rolls

Serves: **4 to 6** ▪ Temperature: **350˚F** ▪ Cooking Time: **8 minutes per batch**

1 (8-ounce) tube of crescent roll dough

⅔ cup semi-sweet or bittersweet chocolate chunks

1 egg white, lightly beaten

¼ cup sliced almonds

powdered sugar, for dusting

butter or oil

1. Pre-heat the air fryer to 350°F.

2. Unwrap the crescent roll dough and separate it into triangles with the points facing away from you. Place a row of chocolate chunks along the bottom edge of the dough. (If you are using chips, make it a double row.) Roll the dough up around the chocolate and then place another row of chunks on the dough. Roll again and finish with one or two chocolate chunks. Be sure to leave the end free of chocolate so that it can adhere to the rest of the roll.

3. Brush the tops of the crescent rolls with the lightly beaten egg white and sprinkle the almonds on top, pressing them into the crescent dough so they adhere.

4. Brush the bottom of the air fryer basket with butter or oil and transfer the crescent rolls to the basket. Air-fry at 350°F for 8 minutes. Remove and let the crescent rolls cool before dusting with powdered sugar and serving.

Easy

Veg

Dress It Up

This recipe allows for lots of variations. Try spreading a little raspberry jam or orange marmalade on the dough before rolling it up around the chocolate for a chocolate raspberry crescent roll. You can even put thinly sliced bananas inside too. Resist the temptation to put too much chocolate in the rolls. I never thought I'd ever write the words "too much" and "chocolate" in the same sentence, but in this case, too much chocolate will cause the dough to fall apart.

Per Serving 340 Calories – 23g Fat (10g Sat. Fat) – 0mg Cholesterol – 36g Carbohydrates – 3g Fiber – 20g Sugar – 5g Protein

Peach Fritters

Makes: **8** ▪ Temperature: **370˚F** ▪ Cooking Time: **6 minutes per batch**

Veg

1½ cups bread flour

1 teaspoon active dry yeast

¼ cup sugar

¼ teaspoon salt

½ cup warm milk

½ teaspoon vanilla extract

2 egg yolks

2 tablespoons melted butter

2 cups small diced peaches
(fresh or frozen)

1 tablespoon butter

1 teaspoon ground cinnamon

1 to 2 tablespoons sugar

Glaze

¾ cup powdered sugar

4 teaspoons milk

1. Combine the flour, yeast, sugar and salt in a bowl. Add the milk, vanilla, egg yolks and melted butter and combine until the dough starts to come together. Transfer the dough to a floured surface and knead it by hand for 2 minutes. Shape the dough into a ball, place it in a large oiled bowl, cover with a clean kitchen towel and let the dough rise in a warm place for 1 to 1½ hours, or until the dough has doubled in size. (See page 61 for a tip on this.)

2. While the dough is rising, melt one tablespoon of butter in a medium saucepan on the stovetop. Add the diced peaches, cinnamon and sugar to taste. Cook the peaches for about 5 minutes, or until they soften. Set the peaches aside to cool.

3. When the dough has risen, transfer it to a floured surface and shape it into a 12-inch circle. Spread the peaches over half of the circle and fold the other half of the dough over the top. With a knife or a board scraper, score the dough by making slits in the dough in a diamond shape. Push the knife straight down into the dough and peaches, rather than slicing through. You should cut through the top layer of dough, but not the bottom. Roll the dough up into a log from one short end to the other. It should be roughly 8 inches long. Some of the peaches will be sticking out of the dough – don't worry, these are supposed to be a little random. Cut the log into 8 equal slices. Place the dough disks on a floured cookie sheet, cover with a clean kitchen towel and let rise in a warm place for 30 minutes.

4. Pre-heat the air fryer to 370°F.

5. Air-fry 2 or 3 fritters at a time at 370°F, for 3 minutes. Flip them over and continue to air-fry for another 2 to 3 minutes, until they are golden brown.

6. Combine the powdered sugar and milk together in a small bowl. Whisk vigorously until smooth. Allow the fritters to cool for at least 10 minutes and then brush the glaze over both the bottom and top of each one. Serve warm or at room temperature.

Per Serving 210 Calories – 4g Fat (2g Sat. Fat) – 55mg Cholesterol –
40g Carbohydrates – 2g Fiber – 20g Sugar – 5g Protein

Step-by-Step Peach Fritters

1. Spread the peaches over half of the circle and fold the other half of the dough over the top.

2. Score the dough by making slits in the dough in a diamond shape. Push the knife straight down and try not to cut through the bottom layer of dough.

3. Roll the dough up into a log, roughly 8 inches long.

4. Cut the log into 8 equal slices.

5. Let the slices rise in a warm place for 30 minutes.

Note from Meredith

You can't really mess these fritters up because they are supposed to be a little messy! Don't fret if the bottom layer of dough gets cut when you score the fritters – just carry on. Don't freak out if some of the peaches fall out of the log when you roll it – just stick them back in. Don't stress if the slices look like they are falling apart – just pick the dough and peaches up, gather them together and place them on a tray to rise. These are not cinnamon rolls, but fritters. Fritters = free form... or freedom!

Baked Eggs with Bacon-Tomato Sauce

Serves: **1** ▪ Temperature: **400˚F** ▪ Cooking Time: **5 + 7 minutes**

GF

1 teaspoon olive oil

2 tablespoons finely chopped onion

1 teaspoon chopped fresh oregano

pinch crushed red pepper flakes

1 (14-ounce) can crushed
or diced tomatoes

salt and freshly ground black pepper

2 slices of bacon, chopped

2 large eggs

¼ cup grated Cheddar cheese

fresh parsley, chopped

1. Start by making the tomato sauce. Pre-heat a medium saucepan over medium heat on the stovetop. Add the olive oil and sauté the onion, oregano and pepper flakes for 5 minutes. Add the tomatoes and bring to a simmer. Season with salt and freshly ground black pepper and simmer for 10 minutes.

2. Meanwhile, pre-heat the air fryer to 400°F and pour a little water into the bottom of the air fryer drawer. (This will help prevent the grease that drips into the bottom drawer from burning and smoking.) Place the bacon in the air fryer basket and air-fry at 400°F for 5 minutes, shaking the basket every once in a while.

3. When the bacon is almost crispy, remove it to a paper-towel lined plate and rinse out the air fryer drawer, draining away the bacon grease.

4. Transfer the tomato sauce to a shallow 7-inch pie dish. Crack the eggs on top of the sauce and scatter the cooked bacon back on top. Season with salt and freshly ground black pepper and transfer the pie dish into the air fryer basket. You can use an aluminum foil sling to help with this by taking a long piece of aluminum foil, folding it in half lengthwise twice until it is roughly 26-inches by 3-inches. Place this under the pie dish and hold the ends of the foil to move the pie dish in and out of the air fryer basket. Tuck the ends of the foil beside the pie dish while it cooks in the air fryer.

5. Air-fry at 400°F for 5 minutes, or until the eggs are almost cooked to your liking. Sprinkle cheese on top and air-fry for an additional 2 minutes. When the cheese has melted, remove the pie dish from the air fryer, sprinkle with a little chopped parsley and let the eggs cool for a few minutes – just enough time to toast some buttered bread in your air fryer!

Prep Help

If you have two pie pans, you can double this recipe and make two orders of baked eggs. The eggs stay so hot in the tomato sauce that you'll have time to make a second batch. You can also speed up the process by using a jarred marinara sauce, but make sure it is warmed before you add the eggs.

Per Serving 470 Calories – 30g Fat (12g Sat. Fat) – 425mg Cholesterol – 24g Carbohydrates – 4g Fiber – 11g Sugar – 24g Protein

Peppered Maple Bacon Knots

Serves: **6** ▪ Temperature: **390˚F** ▪ Cooking Time: **7 to 8 minutes**

GF

1 pound maple smoked center-cut bacon

¼ cup maple syrup

¼ cup brown sugar

coarsely cracked black peppercorns

1. Tie each bacon strip in a loose knot and place them on a baking sheet.

2. Combine the maple syrup and brown sugar in a bowl. Brush each knot generously with this mixture and sprinkle with coarsely cracked black pepper.

3. Pre-heat the air fryer to 390°F.

4. Air-fry the bacon knots in batches. Place one layer of knots in the air fryer basket and air-fry for 5 minutes. Turn the bacon knots over and air-fry for an additional 2 to 3 minutes.

5. Serve warm.

Serving Suggestion

Needless to say, these are a really cute way of serving bacon at a brunch party, but they can also be a delicious little hors d'ouevres at a cocktail party too. The key is to get the right bacon – center cut is the perfect length and thickness for this treat.

Per Serving 410 Calories – 25g Fat (9g Sat. Fat) – 85mg Cholesterol – 17g Carbohydrates – 0g Fiber – 17g Sugar – 19g Protein

Brown Sugar Grapefruit

Serves: **2** ■ Temperature: **400°F** ■ Cooking Time: **4 minutes**

1 grapefruit

2 to 4 teaspoons brown sugar

1. Pre-heat the air fryer to 400°F.

2. While the air fryer is pre-heating, cut the grapefruit in half horizontally (in other words not through the stem or blossom end of the grapefruit). Slice the bottom of the grapefruit to help it sit flat on the counter if necessary. Using a sharp paring knife (serrated is great), cut around the grapefruit between the flesh of the fruit and the peel. Then, cut each segment away from the membrane so that it is sitting freely in the fruit.

3. Sprinkle 1 to 2 teaspoons of brown sugar on each half of the prepared grapefruit. Set up a rack in the air fryer basket (use an air fryer rack or make your own rack with some crumpled up aluminum foil). You don't *have* to use a rack, but doing so will get the grapefruit closer to the element so that the brown sugar can caramelize a little better. Transfer the grapefruit half to the rack in the air fryer basket. Depending on how big your grapefruit are and what size air fryer you have, you may need to do each half separately to make sure they sit flat.

4. Air-fry at 400°F for 4 minutes.

5. Remove and let it cool for just a minute before enjoying.

Prep Help

This grapefruit breakfast couldn't really be easier to prepare. It makes a great start to a winter morning, with a sweet top and a tart-cool bottom. Key to this recipe is keeping the grapefruit chilled and cutting the segments apart before cooking. That way the fruit stays cool and the brown sugar syrup can seep down between the segments. Yum! You can substitute honey or agave syrup or even maple syrup for the brown sugar in this recipe – use whichever flavor you like best. You can also sprinkle a little ground cinnamon on top if you like.

Per Serving 60 Calories – 0g Fat (0g Sat. Fat) – 5mg Cholesterol – 16g Carbohydrates – 2g Fiber – 13g Sugar – 1g Protein

Crustless Broccoli, Roasted Pepper and Fontina Quiche

Serves: **4** ■ Temperature: **360°F** ■ Cooking Time: **60 minutes**

7-inch cake pan

1 cup broccoli florets

¾ cup chopped roasted red peppers

1¼ cups grated Fontina cheese

6 eggs

¾ cup heavy cream

½ teaspoon salt

freshly ground black pepper

1. Pre-heat the air fryer to 360°F.

2. Grease the inside of a 7-inch cake pan (4 inches deep) or other oven-safe pan that will fit into your air fryer. Place the broccoli florets and roasted red peppers in the cake pan and top with the grated Fontina cheese.

3. Whisk the eggs and heavy cream together in a bowl. Season the eggs with salt and freshly ground black pepper. Pour the egg mixture over the cheese and vegetables and cover the pan with aluminum foil. Transfer the cake pan to the air fryer basket.

4. Air-fry at 360°F for 60 minutes. Remove the aluminum foil for the last two minutes of cooking time.

5. Unmold the quiche onto a platter and cut it into slices to serve with a side salad or perhaps some air-fried potatoes.

Roasting Red Peppers

There's no need to *buy* roasted red peppers when roasting them in the air fryer is so easy! Pre-heat the air fryer to 400°F. Place the peppers inside the air fryer basket and air-fry for 18 to 20 minutes, rotating the peppers throughout the cooking time as their skins char. Remove the peppers from the air fryer and cover them with a mixing bowl. This will help the peppers steam and make them much easier to peel once they've cooled. Once cool, pull the stem off the pepper and discard the seeds, which should be attached to the stem. Wipe away any stray seeds. Peel the charred skin away from the pepper, using a finger bowl of water to help clean your fingers throughout the process. Cut the roasted peppers into whatever shape works for your recipe.

Per Serving 410 Calories – 34g Fat (19g Sat. Fat) – 380mg Cholesterol – 6g Carbohydrates – 1g Fiber – 4g Sugar – 20g Protein

Beef

T-bone Steak with Roasted Tomato, Corn and Asparagus Salsa

Serves: **2 to 3** ■ Temperature: **400°F** ■ Cooking Time: **(10 to 15) + 5 minutes**

Easy

GF

1 (20-ounce) T-bone steak

salt and freshly ground black pepper

Salsa

1½ cups cherry tomatoes

¾ cup corn kernels (fresh, or frozen and thawed)

1½ cups sliced asparagus (1-inch slices) (about ½ bunch)

1 tablespoon + 1 teaspoon olive oil, divided

salt and freshly ground black pepper

1½ teaspoons red wine vinegar

3 tablespoons chopped fresh basil

1 tablespoon chopped fresh chives

1. Pre-heat the air fryer to 400°F.

2. Season the steak with salt and pepper and air-fry at 400°F for 10 minutes (medium-rare), 12 minutes (medium), or 15 minutes (well-done), flipping the steak once halfway through the cooking time.

3. In the meantime, toss the tomatoes, corn and asparagus in a bowl with a teaspoon or so of olive oil, salt and freshly ground black pepper.

4. When the steak has finished cooking, remove it to a cutting board, tent loosely with foil and let it rest. Transfer the vegetables to the air fryer and air-fry at 400°F for 5 minutes, shaking the basket once or twice during the cooking process. Transfer the cooked vegetables back into the bowl and toss with the red wine vinegar, remaining olive oil and fresh herbs.

5. To serve, slice the steak on the bias and serve with some of the salsa on top.

Technique Tip

To get faster and more intense browning, elevate the steak in your air fryer basket by putting it on a rack or on some crumpled up aluminum foil.

Per Serving 350 Calories – 14g Fat (3.5g Sat. Fat) – 130mg Cholesterol – 13g Carbohydrates – 3g Fiber – 4g Sugar – 47g Protein

Flank Steak with Roasted Peppers and Chimichurri

Serves: **4** ■ Temperature: **400˚F** ■ Cooking Time: **(8 to 14) + 8 minutes**

Easy

GF

2 cups flat-leaf parsley leaves

¼ cup fresh oregano leaves

3 cloves garlic

½ cup olive oil

¼ cup red wine vinegar

½ teaspoon salt

freshly ground black pepper

¼ teaspoon crushed red pepper flakes

½ teaspoon ground cumin

1 pound flank steak

1 red bell pepper, cut into strips

1 yellow bell pepper, cut into strips

1. Make the chimichurri sauce by chopping the parsley, oregano and garlic in a food processor. Add the olive oil, vinegar and seasonings and process again. Pour half of the sauce into a shallow dish with the flank steak and set the remaining sauce aside. Pierce the flank steak with a needle-style meat tenderizer or a paring knife and marinate the steak for 2 to 24 hours in the refrigerator. When you are ready to cook, remove the steak from the refrigerator and let it sit at room temperature for 30 minutes.

2. Pre-heat the air fryer to 400°F.

3. Cut the flank steak in half so that it fits more easily into the air fryer and transfer both pieces to the air fryer basket. Air-fry for 8 to 14 minutes, depending on how you like your steak cooked (10 minutes will give you medium for a 1-inch thick flank steak). Flip the steak over halfway through the cooking time.

4. When the flank steak is cooked to your liking, transfer it to a cutting board, loosely tent with foil and let it rest while you cook the peppers.

5. Toss the peppers in a little olive oil, salt and freshly ground black pepper and transfer them to the air fryer basket. Air-fry at 400°F for 8 minutes, shaking the basket once or twice throughout the cooking process. To serve, slice the flank steak against the grain of the meat and top with the roasted peppers. Drizzle the reserved chimichurri sauce on top, thinning the sauce with another tablespoon of olive oil if desired.

Note from Meredith

Because no two steaks are identical, cooking steak to your desired degree of doneness requires a little common sense. If you are cooking a very thick flank steak, it will take longer. If you are cooking a very thin flank steak, it will take less time. Using an instant read thermometer, inserted into the center of the steak will help. Medium is around 150°F.

Per Serving 530 Calories – 36g Fat (7g Sat. Fat) – 80mg Cholesterol – 27g Carbohydrates – 11g Fiber – 2g Sugar – 27g Protein

Skirt Steak Fajitas

Serves: 4 ■ Temperature: 400°F ■ Cooking Time: 13 + 17 minutes

2 tablespoons olive oil

¼ cup lime juice

1 clove garlic, minced

½ teaspoon ground cumin

½ teaspoon hot sauce

½ teaspoon salt

2 tablespoons chopped fresh cilantro

1 pound skirt steak

1 onion, sliced

1 teaspoon chili powder

1 red pepper, sliced

1 green pepper, sliced

salt and freshly ground black pepper

8 flour tortillas

shredded lettuce, crumbled Queso Fresco (or grated Cheddar cheese), sliced black olives, diced tomatoes, sour cream and guacamole for serving

1. Combine the olive oil, lime juice, garlic, cumin, hot sauce, salt and cilantro in a shallow dish. Add the skirt steak and turn it over several times to coat all sides. Pierce the steak with a needle-style meat tenderizer or paring knife. Marinate the steak in the refrigerator for at least 3 hours, or overnight. When you are ready to cook, remove the steak from the refrigerator and let it sit at room temperature for 30 minutes.

2. Pre-heat the air fryer to 400°F.

3. Toss the onion slices with the chili powder and a little olive oil and transfer them to the air fryer basket. Air-fry at 400°F for 5 minutes. Add the red and green peppers to the air fryer basket with the onions, season with salt and pepper and air-fry for 8 more minutes, until the onions and peppers are soft. Transfer the vegetables to a dish and cover with aluminum foil to keep warm.

4. Place the skirt steak in the air fryer basket and pour the marinade over the top. Air-fry at 400°F for 12 minutes. Flip the steak over and air-fry at 400°F for an additional 5 minutes. (The time needed for your steak will depend on the thickness of the skirt steak. 17 minutes should bring your steak to roughly medium.) Transfer the cooked steak to a cutting board and let the steak rest for a few minutes. If the peppers and onions need to be heated, return them to the air fryer for just 1 to 2 minutes.

5. Thinly slice the steak at an angle, cutting against the grain of the steak. Serve the steak with the onions and peppers, the warm tortillas and the fajita toppings on the side so that everyone can make their own fajita.

Prep Help
Skirt steak has incredible flavor, but it needs to be marinated and tenderized. To avoid a tough, chewy result, skirt steak should be cooked medium-rare and still pink inside to no more than 140°F.

Per Serving 470 Calories – 22g Fat (6g Sat. Fat) – 80mg Cholesterol – 39g Carbohydrates – 4g Fiber – 5g Sugar – 28g Protein

Balsamic Marinated Rib Eye Steak with Balsamic Fried Cipollini Onions

Serves: 2 ■ Temperature: 400°F ■ Cooking Time: (12 to 16) + 10 minutes

Easy

GF

3 tablespoons balsamic vinegar

2 cloves garlic, sliced

1 tablespoon Dijon mustard

1 teaspoon fresh thyme leaves

1 (16-ounce) boneless rib eye steak

coarsely ground black pepper

salt

1 (8-ounce) bag cipollini onions, peeled

1 teaspoon balsamic vinegar

1. Combine the 3 tablespoons of balsamic vinegar, garlic, Dijon mustard and thyme in a small bowl. Pour this marinade over the steak. Pierce the steak several times with a paring knife or a needle-style meat tenderizer and season it generously with coarsely ground black pepper. Flip the steak over and pierce the other side in a similar fashion, seasoning again with the coarsely ground black pepper. Marinate the steak for 2 to 24 hours in the refrigerator. When you are ready to cook, remove the steak from the refrigerator and let it sit at room temperature for 30 minutes.

2. Pre-heat the air fryer to 400°F.

3. Season the steak with salt and air-fry at 400°F for 12 minutes (medium-rare), 14 minutes (medium), or 16 minutes (well-done), flipping the steak once half way through the cooking time.

4. While the steak is air-frying, toss the onions with 1 teaspoon of balsamic vinegar and season with salt.

5. Remove the steak from the air fryer and let it rest while you fry the onions. Transfer the onions to the air fryer basket and air-fry for 10 minutes, adding a few more minutes if your onions are very large. Then, slice the steak on the bias and serve with the fried onions on top.

Substitution Tip

If you can't find cipollini onions, you can use pearl onions or even a regular Spanish onion, sliced or cut into chunks.

Per Serving 410 Calories – 19g Fat (7g Sat. Fat) – 145g Cholesterol – 10g Carbohydrates – 1g Fiber – 4g Sugar – 50g Protein

Beef and Spinach Braciole

Serves: 4 ■ Temperature: 400°F + 350°F + 250°F ■ Cooking Time: 20 + 12 + 60 minutes

7-inch oven-safe baking pan or casserole

½ onion, finely chopped

1 teaspoon olive oil

⅓ cup red wine

2 cups crushed tomatoes

1 teaspoon Italian seasoning

½ teaspoon garlic powder

¼ teaspoon crushed red pepper flakes

2 tablespoons chopped fresh parsley

2 top round steaks (about 1½ pounds)

salt and freshly ground black pepper

2 cups fresh spinach, chopped

1 clove minced garlic

½ cup roasted red peppers, julienned

½ cup grated pecorino cheese

¼ cup pine nuts, toasted and rough chopped

2 tablespoons olive oil

1. Pre-heat the air fryer to 400°F.

2. Toss the onions and olive oil together in a 7-inch metal baking pan or casserole dish. Air-fry at 400°F for 5 minutes, stirring a couple times during the cooking process. Add the red wine, crushed tomatoes, Italian seasoning, garlic powder, red pepper flakes and parsley and stir. Cover the pan tightly with aluminum foil, lower the air fryer temperature to 350°F and continue to air-fry for 15 minutes.

3. While the sauce is simmering, prepare the beef. Using a meat mallet, pound the beef until it is ¼-inch thick. Season both sides of the beef with salt and pepper. Combine the spinach, garlic, red peppers, pecorino cheese, pine nuts and olive oil in a medium bowl. Season with salt and freshly ground black pepper. Spread the mixture evenly over the steaks. Starting at one of the short ends, roll the beef around the filling, tucking in the sides as you roll to ensure the filling is completely enclosed. Secure the beef rolls with toothpicks.

4. Remove the baking pan with the sauce from the air fryer and set it aside. Pre-heat the air fryer to 400°F.

5. Brush or spray the beef rolls with a little olive oil and air-fry at 400°F for 12 minutes, rotating the beef during the cooking process for even browning. When the beef is browned, submerge the rolls into the sauce in the baking pan, cover the pan with foil and return it to the air fryer. Air-fry at 250°F for 60 minutes.

6. Remove the beef rolls from the sauce. Cut each roll into slices and serve with pasta, ladling some of the sauce overtop.

Preparation Tip

The trickiest part of this recipe is getting the top round steaks thin enough to roll them around the filling. If you're getting your beef from a butcher, you could ask him or her to pound the steaks out for you. If you don't have a butcher, you can get out all your frustrations pounding this meat – much cheaper than therapy!

Per Serving 260 Calories – 17g Fat (4g Sat. Fat) – 20mg Cholesterol – 15g Carbohydrates – 3g Fiber – 7g Sugar – 12g Protein

Rib Eye Cheesesteaks with Fried Onions

Serves: **2** ■ Temperature: **400°F** ■ Cooking Time: **20 minutes**

1 (12-ounce) rib eye steak

2 tablespoons Worcestershire sauce

salt and freshly ground black pepper

½ onion, sliced

2 tablespoons butter, melted

4 ounces sliced Cheddar or provolone cheese

2 long hoagie rolls, lightly toasted

1. Place the steak in the freezer for 30 minutes to make it easier to slice. When it is well-chilled, thinly slice the steak against the grain and transfer it to a bowl. Pour the Worcestershire sauce over the steak and season it with salt and pepper. Allow the meat to come to room temperature.

2. Pre-heat the air fryer to 400°F.

3. Toss the sliced onion with the butter and transfer it to the air fryer basket. Air-fry at 400°F for 12 minutes, shaking the basket a few times during the cooking process. Place the steak on top of the onions and air-fry for another 6 minutes, stirring the meat and onions together halfway through the cooking time.

4. When the air fryer has finished cooking, divide the steak and onions in half in the air fryer basket, pushing each half to one side of the air fryer basket. Place the cheese on top of each half, push the drawer back into the turned off air fryer and let it sit for 2 minutes, until the cheese has melted.

5. Transfer each half of the cheesesteak mixture into a toasted roll with the cheese side up and dig in!

Dress It Up

This is a recipe for a basic cheesesteak with onions, but you can make it your own by adding other toppings like mushrooms or sliced peppers. Just air-fry them along with the onions before you add the steak.

Per Serving 780 Calories - 44g Fat (23g Sat. Fat) - 175mg Cholesterol - 38g Carbohydrates - 1g Fiber - 5g Sugar - 58g Protein

The Perfect Burger

Everyone has an image of the perfect burger. My perfect burger has a nicely browned crust with a tasty and juicy interior. It's tender, not tough or chewy and is juicy but not dripping with fat. Once you've prepared the burger patty the right way, the air fryer is a great way to cook the perfect burger. The fat can drip away from the patty through the perforated basket and into the drawer below, the intense heat from above gives the burger a nice brown crust and the high speed of cooking with contained convection heat makes it much easier to end up with a juicy interior, no matter how you like your burger cooked. Here are a few tips to help you make the perfect burgers in your air fryer.

■ **Start with the right meat.** If you are making a beef burger, choose ground chuck, which has great flavor and look for 80% lean meat. The fat content is important for a tasty, moist burger. Any more than 20% fat makes the burger greasy, and any less fat will make the burger a little dry.

■ **Season with salt and pepper** when you mix the burger meat, before you shape them into patties. Seasoning just the surface of the meat as you cook the patties will make the outside of the burger taste great, but leave the inside of the burger a little bland. It's important to season throughout the process.

■ **Shape the burger gently.** Over-handling will create a burger patty that is dense and tough. If you're adding ingredients to the burger meat, mix it in as gently as you can. Packing the meat by tossing it back and forth from one hand to another [rather than squeezing the meat] packs the burger well without over-mixing. Giving your burger straight sides by flattening the edges with your hands will allow you to fit more burgers into the air fryer basket at one time.

■ **Dent your patties.** Make an indentation in the center of the burger patty so that it looks something like a donut. This indentation will create a burger that is flat when fully cooked, rather than a round baseball-like burger.

■ **Add water to the air fryer drawer.** Adding water to the drawer underneath the basket helps prevent grease from getting too hot and smoking. (You should also do this when cooking bacon, sausage, even roasts if they are particularly fatty.)

■ **Remember to flip.** Just as you would on a grill or in a skillet, remember to flip your burger halfway through the cooking time to cook it evenly and brown on both sides.

■ **Use toothpicks to hold foods down.** Every once in a while, the fan from the air fryer will pick up light foods and blow them around. If you're topping your burger with a slice of cheese, secure the cheese slice to the burger with a toothpick or two.

■ **Give it a rest!** As with all meats, resting the patties for just a few minutes will result in a juicer burger. Sometimes, preparing all the fixings on your burger bun is all the time you need!

Bourbon Bacon Burgers

Serves: 2 ■ Temperature: 390°F + 370°F ■ Cooking Time: 8 + (15 to 20) minutes

Easy

1 tablespoon bourbon

2 tablespoons brown sugar

3 strips maple bacon, cut in half

¾ pound ground beef (80% lean)

1 tablespoon minced onion

2 tablespoons BBQ sauce

½ teaspoon salt

freshly ground black pepper

2 slices Colby Jack cheese
(or Monterey Jack)

2 Kaiser rolls

lettuce and tomato, for serving

Zesty Burger Sauce:

2 tablespoons BBQ sauce

2 tablespoons mayonnaise

¼ teaspoon ground paprika

freshly ground black pepper

1. Pre-heat the air fryer to 390°F and pour a little water into the bottom of the air fryer drawer. (This will help prevent the grease that drips into the bottom drawer from burning and smoking.)

2. Combine the bourbon and brown sugar in a small bowl. Place the bacon strips in the air fryer basket and brush with the brown sugar mixture. Air-fry at 390°F for 4 minutes. Flip the bacon over, brush with more brown sugar and air-fry at 390°F for an additional 4 minutes until crispy.

3. While the bacon is cooking, make the burger patties. Combine the ground beef, onion, BBQ sauce, salt and pepper in a large bowl. Mix together thoroughly with your hands and shape the meat into 2 patties.

4. Transfer the burger patties to the air fryer basket and air-fry the burgers at 370°F for 15 to 20 minutes, depending on how you like your burger cooked (15 minutes for rare to medium-rare; 20 minutes for well-done). Flip the burgers over halfway through the cooking process.

5. While the burgers are air-frying, make the burger sauce by combining the BBQ sauce, mayonnaise, paprika and freshly ground black pepper in a bowl.

6. When the burgers are cooked to your liking, top each patty with a slice of Colby Jack cheese and air-fry for an additional minute, just to melt the cheese. (You might want to pin the cheese slice to the burger with a toothpick to prevent it from blowing off in your air fryer.) Spread the sauce on the inside of the Kaiser rolls, place the burgers on the rolls, top with the bourbon bacon, lettuce and tomato and enjoy!

Per Serving
Burger Without Burger Sauce 900 Calories – 52g Fat (21g Sat. Fat) – 180mg Cholesterol – 53g Carbohydrates – 3g Fiber – 21g Sugar – 47g Protein
Burger Sauce 60 Calories – 3.5g Fat (0.5g Sat. Fat) – 5mg Cholesterol – 6g Carbohydrates – 0g Fiber – 5g Sugar – 0g Protein

Brie and Cranberry Burgers

Serves: **3 or 4** ■ Temperature: **390˚F** ■ Cooking Time: **9 minutes**

Easy

1 pound ground beef (80% lean)

1 tablespoon chopped fresh thyme

1 tablespoon Worcestershire sauce

½ teaspoon salt

freshly ground black pepper

1 (4-ounce) wheel of Brie cheese, sliced

handful of arugula

3 or 4 brioche hamburger buns
(or potato hamburger buns), toasted

¼ to ½ cup whole berry cranberry sauce

1. Combine the beef, thyme, Worcestershire sauce, salt and pepper together in a large bowl and mix well. Divide the meat into 4 (¼-pound) portions or 3 larger portions and then form them into burger patties, being careful not to over-handle the meat.

2. Pre-heat the air fryer to 390°F and pour a little water into the bottom of the air fryer drawer. (This will help prevent the grease that drips into the bottom drawer from burning and smoking.)

3. Transfer the burgers to the air fryer basket. Air-fry the burgers at 390°F for 5 minutes. Flip the burgers over and air-fry for another 2 minutes. Top each burger with a couple slices of brie and air-fry for another minute or two, just to soften the cheese.

4. Build the burgers by placing a few leaves of arugula on the bottom bun, adding the burger and a spoonful of cranberry sauce on top. Top with the other half of the hamburger bun and enjoy.

Timing Tip

The timing of this recipe depends on how thick you make the burgers. If cooking four quarter-pound burgers at one time, the time above should give you burgers that are medium to medium-well done. If you like your burgers a little less cooked, subtract a minute or two.

Per Serving 630 Calories – 38g Fat (15g Sat. Fat) – 165mg Cholesterol – 39g Carbohydrates – 1g Fiber – 10g Sugar – 31g Protein

Vietnamese Beef Lettuce Wraps

Serves: **4** ■ Temperature: **400°F** ■ Cooking Time: **12 minutes**

GF*

⅓ cup low-sodium soy sauce*

2 teaspoons fish sauce*

2 teaspoons brown sugar

1 tablespoon chili paste

juice of 1 lime

2 cloves garlic, minced

2 teaspoons fresh ginger, minced

1 pound beef sirloin

Sauce

⅓ cup low-sodium soy sauce*

juice of 2 limes

1 tablespoon mirin wine

2 teaspoons chili paste

Serving

1 head butter lettuce

½ cup julienned carrots

½ cup julienned cucumber

½ cup sliced radishes,
sliced into half moons

2 cups cooked rice noodles

⅓ cup chopped peanuts

*Make this recipe gluten free by using
a gluten-free soy sauce and fish sauce.

1. Combine the soy sauce, fish sauce, brown sugar, chili paste, lime juice, garlic and ginger in a bowl. Slice the beef into thin slices, then cut those slices in half. Add the beef to the marinade and marinate for 1 to 3 hours in the refrigerator. When you are ready to cook, remove the steak from the refrigerator and let it sit at room temperature for 30 minutes.

2. Pre-heat the air fryer to 400°F.

3. Transfer the beef and marinade to the air fryer basket. Air-fry at 400°F for 12 minutes, shaking the basket a few times during the cooking process.

4. While the beef is cooking, prepare a wrap-building station. Combine the soy sauce, lime juice, mirin wine and chili paste in a bowl and transfer to a little pouring vessel. Separate the lettuce leaves from the head of lettuce and put them in a serving bowl. Place the carrots, cucumber, radish, rice noodles and chopped peanuts all in separate serving bowls.

5. When the beef has finished cooking, transfer it to another serving bowl and invite your guests to build their wraps. To build the wraps, place some beef in a lettuce leaf and top with carrots, cucumbers, some rice noodles and chopped peanuts. Drizzle a little sauce over top, fold the lettuce around the ingredients and enjoy!

Substitution Tip
If you can't find mirin (Japanese sweet rice wine), you can use 1 tablespoon of white wine, vermouth or dry sherry, along with ½ teaspoon of sugar.

Per Serving 380 Calories – 11g Fat (2.5g Sat. Fat) – 80mg Cholesterol –
37g Carbohydrates – 3g Fiber – 7g Sugar – 34g Protein

Meatloaf with Tangy Tomato Glaze

Serves: 6 ■ Temperature: 350°F ■ Cooking Time: 45 to 50 minutes

GF*

1 pound ground beef

½ pound ground pork

½ pound ground veal (or turkey)

1 medium onion, diced

1 small clove of garlic, minced

2 egg yolks, lightly beaten

½ cup tomato ketchup

1 tablespoon Worcestershire sauce

½ cup plain breadcrumbs*

2 teaspoons salt

freshly ground black pepper

½ cup chopped fresh parsley,
plus more for garnish

6 tablespoons ketchup

1 tablespoon balsamic vinegar

2 tablespoons brown sugar

* Make this meatloaf gluten free by
using gluten-free breadcrumbs.

1. Combine the meats, onion, garlic, egg yolks, ketchup, Worcestershire sauce, breadcrumbs, salt, pepper and fresh parsley in a large bowl and mix well.

2. Pre-heat the air fryer to 350°F and pour a little water into the bottom of the air fryer drawer. (This will help prevent the grease that drips into the bottom drawer from burning and smoking.)

3. Transfer the meatloaf mixture to the air fryer basket, packing it down gently. Run a spatula around the meatloaf to create a space about ½-inch wide between the meat and the side of the air fryer basket.

4. Air-fry at 350°F for 20 minutes. Carefully invert the meatloaf onto a plate (remember to remove the basket from the air fryer drawer so you don't pour all the grease out) and slide it back into the air fryer basket to turn it over. Re-shape the meatloaf with a spatula if necessary. Air-fry for another 20 minutes at 350°F.

5. Combine the ketchup, balsamic vinegar and brown sugar in a bowl and spread the mixture over the meatloaf. Air-fry for another 5 to 10 minutes, until an instant read thermometer inserted into the center of the meatloaf registers 160°F.

6. Allow the meatloaf to rest for a few more minutes and then transfer it to a serving platter using a spatula. Slice the meatloaf, sprinkle a little chopped parsley on top if desired, and serve.

Note from Meredith
The air fryer is a pretty perfect appliance for meatloaf! The perforated basket allows the grease to drip down away from the meat into the bottom drawer, leaving the meat to roast and cook up above, and the top down heat of the air fryer gives the meatloaf a beautiful glaze at the end.

Per Serving 370 Calories – 21g Fat (8g Sat. Fat) – 165mg Cholesterol – 15g Carbohydrates – 1g Fiber – 8g Sugar – 30g Protein

Mongolian Beef

Easy

GF*

1½ pounds flank steak, thinly sliced on the bias into ¼-inch strips

Marinade

2 tablespoons soy sauce*

1 clove garlic, smashed

big pinch crushed red pepper flakes

Sauce

1 tablespoon vegetable oil

2 cloves garlic, minced

1 tablespoon finely grated fresh ginger

3 dried red chili peppers

¾ cup soy sauce*

¾ cup chicken stock

5 to 6 tablespoons brown sugar (depending on how sweet you want the sauce)

½ cup cornstarch, divided

1 bunch scallions, sliced into 2-inch pieces

*Make this recipe gluten free by using a gluten-free soy sauce.

1. Marinate the beef in the soy sauce, garlic and red pepper flakes for one hour.

2. In the meantime, make the sauce. Pre-heat a small sauce-pan over medium heat on the stovetop. Add the oil, garlic, ginger and dried chili peppers and sauté for just a minute or two. Add the soy sauce, chicken stock and brown sugar and continue to simmer for a few minutes. Dissolve 3 tablespoons of cornstarch in 3 tablespoons of water and stir this into the saucepan. Stir the sauce over medium heat until it thickens. Set this aside.

3. Pre-heat the air fryer to 400°F.

4. Remove the beef from the marinade and transfer it to a zipper sealable plastic bag with the remaining cornstarch. Shake it around to completely coat the beef and transfer the coated strips of beef to a baking sheet or plate, shaking off any excess cornstarch. Spray the strips with vegetable oil on all sides and transfer them to the air fryer basket.

5. Air-fry at 400°F for 15 minutes, shaking the basket to toss and rotate the beef strips throughout the cooking process. Add the scallions for the last 4 minutes of the cooking. Transfer the hot beef strips and scallions to a bowl and toss with the sauce (warmed on the stovetop if necessary), coating all the beef strips with the sauce. Serve warm over white rice.

Technique Tip

You can also cook this beef in two batches to get more even browning. It will take roughly 6 minutes per batch. Then, throw it all together in the air fryer for another minute or two to heat everything up together before saucing it up.

Per Serving 380 Calories – 15g Fat (5g Sat. Fat) – 135mg Cholesterol – 21g Carbohydrates – 0g Fiber – 16g Sugar – 39g Protein

Air-Fried Roast Beef with Rosemary Roasted Potatoes

Serves: **8 to 10** ▪ Temperature: **360˚F** ▪ Cooking Time: **60 minutes**

1 (5-pound) top sirloin roast

salt and freshly ground black pepper

1 teaspoon dried thyme

2 pounds red potatoes, halved or quartered

2 teaspoons olive oil

1 teaspoon very finely chopped fresh rosemary, plus more for garnish

GF

1. Start by making sure your roast will fit into the air fryer basket without touching the top element. Trim it if you have to in order to get it to fit nicely in your air fryer. (You can always save the trimmings for another use, like a beef sandwich.)

2. Pre-heat the air fryer to 360°F.

3. Season the beef all over with salt, pepper and thyme. Transfer the seasoned roast to the air fryer basket.

4. Air-fry at 360°F for 20 minutes. Turn the roast over and continue to air-fry at 360°F for another 20 minutes.

5. Toss the potatoes with the olive oil, salt, pepper and fresh rosemary. Turn the roast over again in the air fryer basket and toss the potatoes in around the sides of the roast. Air-fry the roast and potatoes at 360°F for another 20 minutes. Check the internal temperature of the roast with an instant-read thermometer, and continue to roast until the beef is 5° lower than your desired degree of doneness. (Rare – 130°F, Medium – 150°F, Well done – 170°F.) Let the roast rest for 5 to 10 minutes before slicing and serving. While the roast is resting, continue to air-fry the potatoes if desired for extra browning and crispiness.

6. Slice the roast and serve with the potatoes, adding a little more fresh rosemary if desired.

Shopping Tip
Buying the perfect cut of beef to roast can be the secret to your success. The tenderloin roast, ribeye roast or strip roast are considered the best, but they have a hefty price tag too. The top sirloin or tri-tip roasts are two more economical options, and any of these cuts can be roasted successfully. If you're cooking a roast smaller than 5 pounds, time it so that you're cooking for roughly 12 minutes per pound to get to medium.

Per Serving 360 Calories – 11g Fat (3.5g Sat. Fat) – 175mg Cholesterol – 7g Carbohydrates – 1g Fiber – 1g Sugar – 59g Protein

Pork & Lamb

Kielbasa Sausage with Pierogies and Caramelized Onions

Serves: **3 to 4** ■ Temperature: **400°F** ■ Cooking Time: **30 minutes**

Easy

1 Vidalia or sweet onion, sliced

olive oil

salt and freshly ground black pepper

2 tablespoons butter, cut into small cubes

1 teaspoon sugar

1 pound light Polish kielbasa sausage, cut into 2-inch chunks

1 (13-ounce) package frozen mini pierogies

2 teaspoons vegetable or olive oil

chopped scallions

1. Pre-heat the air fryer to 400°F.

2. Toss the sliced onions with a little olive oil, salt and pepper and transfer them to the air fryer basket. Dot the onions with pieces of butter and air-fry at 400°F for 2 minutes. Then sprinkle the sugar over the onions and stir. Pour any melted butter from the bottom of the air fryer drawer over the onions (do this over the sink – some of the butter will spill through the basket). Continue to air-fry for another 13 minutes, stirring or shaking the basket every few minutes to cook the onions evenly.

3. Add the kielbasa chunks to the onions and toss. Air-fry for another 5 minutes, shaking the basket halfway through the cooking time. Transfer the kielbasa and onions to a bowl and cover with aluminum foil to keep warm.

4. Toss the frozen pierogies with the vegetable or olive oil and transfer them to the air fryer basket. Air-fry at 400°F for 8 minutes, shaking the basket twice during the cooking time.

5. When the pierogies have finished cooking, return the kielbasa and onions to the air fryer and gently toss with the pierogies. Air-fry for 2 more minutes and then transfer everything to a serving platter. Garnish with the chopped scallions and serve hot with the spicy sour cream sauce below.

Spicy Sour Cream Sauce

½ cup light sour cream

2 tablespoons Dijon mustard

2 teaspoons prepared horseradish

1. Combine the sour cream, Dijon mustard and horseradish in a small bowl, whisking until smooth.

Note from Meredith
I enjoy eating kielbasa with mustard and love sour cream on pierogies. By combining these two ingredients, you can make a quick and easy sauce for this dish.

Per Serving
Keilbasa and Pierogies 590 Calories – 42g Fat (14g Sat. Fat) – 95mg Cholesterol – 35g Carbohydrates – 3g Fiber – 5g Sugar – 17g Protein
Spicy Sour Cream Sauce 45 Calories – 3g Fat (2g Sat. Fat) – 10mg Cholesterol – 2g Carbohydrates – 0g Fiber – 0g Sugar – 1g Protein

Crispy Pork Medallions
with Radicchio and Endive Salad

Serves: 4 ▪ Temperature: 400°F ▪ Cooking Time: **7 minutes per batch**

Easy

1 (8-ounce) pork tenderloin

salt and freshly ground black pepper

¼ cup flour

2 eggs, lightly beaten

¾ cup cracker meal

1 teaspoon paprika

1 teaspoon dry mustard

1 teaspoon garlic powder

1 teaspoon dried thyme

1 teaspoon salt

vegetable or canola oil, in spray bottle

Vinaigrette

¼ cup white balsamic vinegar

2 tablespoons agave syrup
(or honey or maple syrup)

1 tablespoon Dijon mustard

juice of ½ lemon

2 tablespoons chopped chervil
or flat-leaf parsley

salt and freshly ground black pepper

½ cup extra-virgin olive oil

Radicchio and Endive Salad

1 heart romaine lettuce,
torn into large pieces

½ head radicchio, coarsely chopped

2 heads endive, sliced

½ cup cherry tomatoes, halved

3 ounces fresh mozzarella, diced

salt and freshly ground black pepper

1. Slice the pork tenderloin into 1-inch slices. Using a meat pounder, pound the pork slices into thin ½-inch medallions. Generously season the pork with salt and freshly ground black pepper on both sides.

2. Set up a dredging station using three shallow dishes. Place the flour in one dish and the beaten eggs in a second dish. Combine the cracker meal, paprika, dry mustard, garlic powder, thyme and salt in a third dish.

3. Pre-heat the air fryer to 400°F.

4. Dredge the pork medallions in flour first and then into the beaten egg. Let the excess egg drip off and coat both sides of the medallions with the cracker meal crumb mixture. Spray both sides of the coated medallions with vegetable or canola oil.

5. Air-fry the medallions in two batches at 400°F for 5 minutes. Once you have air-fried all the medallions, flip them all over and return the first batch of medallions back into the air fryer on top of the second batch. Air-fry at 400°F for an additional 2 minutes.

6. While the medallions are cooking, make the salad and dressing. Whisk the white balsamic vinegar, agave syrup, Dijon mustard, lemon juice, chervil, salt and pepper together in a small bowl. Whisk in the olive oil slowly until combined and thickened.

7. Combine the romaine lettuce, radicchio, endive, cherry tomatoes, and mozzarella cheese in a large salad bowl. Drizzle the dressing over the vegetables and toss to combine. Season with salt and freshly ground black pepper.

8. Serve the pork medallions warm on or beside the salad.

Did You Know?
Chervil is also known as French parsley. It has hints of licorice or anise and gives this dressing a nice tangy flavor. It you can't find it, flat leaf parsley will work in its place.

Per Serving 500 Calories – 36g Fat (8g Sat. Fat) – 90mg Cholesterol –
27g Carbohydrates – 11g Fiber – 8g Sugar – 24g Protein

Pork Taco Gorditas

Serves: 4 ■ Temperature: 400°F + 380°F ■ Cooking Time: 11 minutes + 10 minutes per batch

1 pound lean ground pork

2 tablespoons chili powder

2 tablespoons ground cumin

1 teaspoon dried oregano

2 teaspoons paprika

1 teaspoon garlic powder

½ cup water

1 (15-ounce) can pinto beans, drained and rinsed

½ cup taco sauce

salt and freshly ground black pepper

2 cups grated Cheddar cheese

5 (12-inch) flour tortillas

4 (8-inch) crispy corn tortilla shells

4 cups shredded lettuce

1 tomato, diced

⅓ cup sliced black olives

sour cream, for serving

tomato salsa, for serving

1. Pre-heat the air fryer to 400°F.

2. Place the ground pork in the air fryer basket and air-fry at 400°F for 10 minutes, stirring a few times during the cooking process to gently break up the meat. Combine the chili powder, cumin, oregano, paprika, garlic powder and water in a small bowl. Stir the spice mixture into the browned pork. Stir in the beans and taco sauce and air-fry for an additional minute. Transfer the pork mixture to a bowl. Season to taste with salt and freshly ground black pepper.

3. Sprinkle ½ cup of the shredded cheese in the center of four of the flour tortillas, making sure to leave a 2-inch border around the edge free of cheese and filling. Divide the pork mixture among the four tortillas, placing it on top of the cheese. Place a crunchy corn tortilla on top of the pork and top with shredded lettuce, diced tomatoes, and black olives. Cut the remaining flour tortilla into 4 quarters. These quarters of tortilla will serve as the bottom of the gordita. Place one quarter tortilla on top of each gordita and fold the edges of the bottom flour tortilla up over the sides, enclosing the filling. While holding the seams down, brush the bottom of the gordita with olive oil and place the seam side down on the countertop while you finish the remaining three gorditas.

4. Pre-heat the air fryer to 380°F.

5. Air-fry one gordita at a time. Transfer the gordita carefully to the air fryer basket, seam side down. Brush or spray the top tortilla with oil and air-fry for 5 minutes. Carefully turn the gordita over and air-fry for an additional 4 to 5 minutes, until both sides are browned. When finished air frying all four gorditas, layer them back into the air fryer for an additional minute to make sure they are all warm before serving with sour cream and salsa.

Per Serving 670 Calories – 30g Fat (12g Sat. Fat) – 115mg Cholesterol – 59g Carbohydrates – 13g Fiber – 4g Sugar – 48g Protein

Step-by-Step Gorditas

1. Sprinkle ½ cup of the shredded cheese in the center of the tortilla. Place the pork mixture on top of the cheese.

2. Place a crunchy corn tortilla on top of the pork.

3. Top with shredded lettuce, diced tomatoes and black olives.

4. Place a quarter of a tortilla on top and fold the edges of the bottom tortilla up over the sides, enclosing the filling.

5. Hold the seams down and brush the bottom of the gordita with olive oil.

Did You Know?

A gordita in Mexican cuisine is a pastry made with masa (corn flour dough), which is then stuffed with cheese and other ingredients. This recipe uses flour tortillas instead of corn pastry, and adds a little crunch by including a crispy corn tortilla in the center. You can find crispy tortillas in your grocery store, or you can crisp one yourself by brushing a corn tortilla with oil and air-frying it for a few minutes, turning it as it cooks.

125

Almond and Sun-dried Tomato Crusted Pork Chops

Serves: 4 ■ Temperature: 370˚F ■ Cooking Time: **10 minutes**

½ cup oil-packed sun-dried tomatoes

½ cup toasted almonds

¼ cup grated Parmesan cheese

½ cup olive oil

2 tablespoons water

½ teaspoon salt

freshly ground black pepper

4 center-cut boneless pork chops (about 1¼ pounds)

1. Place the sun-dried tomatoes into a food processor and pulse them until they are coarsely chopped. Add the almonds, Parmesan cheese, olive oil, water, salt and pepper. Process all the ingredients into a smooth paste. Spread most of the paste (leave a little in reserve) onto both sides of the pork chops and then pierce the meat several times with a needle-style meat tenderizer or a fork. Let the pork chops sit and marinate for at least 1 hour (refrigerate if marinating for longer than 1 hour).

2. Pre-heat the air fryer to 370°F.

3. Brush a little olive oil on the bottom of the air fryer basket. Transfer the pork chops into the air fryer basket, spooning a little more of the sun-dried tomato paste onto the pork chops if there are any gaps where the paste may have been rubbed off. Air-fry the pork chops at 370°F for 10 minutes, turning the chops over halfway through the cooking process.

4. When the pork chops have finished cooking, transfer them to a serving plate and serve with mashed potatoes and vegetables for a hearty meal.

Easy
GF

Substitution Tip
You can certainly use a bone-in pork chop for this recipe if you'd prefer. It will have even more flavor, but you might not be able to fit all four pork chops in the air fryer in one batch.

Per Serving 560 Calories – 44g Fat (8g Sat. Fat) – 80mg Cholesterol – 6g Carbohydrates – 2g Fiber – 3g Sugar – 34g Protein

Orange Glazed Pork Tenderloin

Serves: **3 to 4** ■ Temperature: **370°F** ■ Cooking Time: **23 minutes**

Easy

GF*

2 tablespoons brown sugar

2 teaspoons cornstarch

2 teaspoons Dijon mustard

½ cup orange juice

½ teaspoon soy sauce*

2 teaspoons grated fresh ginger

¼ cup white wine

zest of 1 orange

1 pound pork tenderloin

salt and freshly ground black pepper

oranges, halved (for garnish)

fresh parsley or other green herb
(for garnish)

*Make this recipe gluten free by using
a gluten-free soy sauce.

1. Combine the brown sugar, cornstarch, Dijon mustard, orange juice, soy sauce, ginger, white wine and orange zest in a small saucepan and bring the mixture to a boil on the stovetop. Lower the heat and simmer while you cook the pork tenderloin or until the sauce has thickened.

2. Pre-heat the air fryer to 370°F.

3. Season all sides of the pork tenderloin with salt and freshly ground black pepper. Transfer the tenderloin to the air fryer basket, bending the pork into a wide "U" shape if necessary to fit in the basket. Air-fry at 370°F for 20 to 23 minutes, or until the internal temperature reaches 145°F. Flip the tenderloin over halfway through the cooking process and baste with the sauce.

4. Transfer the tenderloin to a cutting board and let it rest for 5 minutes. Slice the pork at a slight angle and serve immediately with orange halves and fresh herbs to dress it up. Drizzle any remaining glaze over the top.

Dress It Up
This pork tenderloin cooks so quickly in the air fryer that it won't have a lot of time to get really brown, but it will be super moist and tender. Dress it up with the glaze, oranges and herbs to make a prettier presentation.

Per Serving 190 Calories – 2.5g Fat (1g Sat. Fat) – 75mg Cholesterol –
12g Carbohydrates – 1g Fiber – 9g Sugar – 24g Protein

Blackberry BBQ Glazed Country-Style Ribs

Serves: **2** ■ Temperature: **330°F** ■ Cooking Time: **40 minutes**

Easy

GF*

½ cup + 2 tablespoons sherry or Madeira wine, divided

1 pound boneless country-style pork ribs

salt and freshly ground black pepper

1 tablespoon Chinese 5-spice powder

¼ cup blackberry preserves

¼ cup hoisin sauce*

1 clove garlic, minced

1 generous tablespoon grated fresh ginger

2 scallions, chopped

1 tablespoon sesame seeds, toasted

*Make this recipe gluten free by using a gluten-free hoisin sauce.

1. Pre-heat the air fryer to 330°F and pour ½ cup of the sherry into the bottom of the air fryer drawer.

2. Season the ribs with salt, pepper and the 5-spice powder.

3. Air-fry the ribs at 330°F for 20 minutes, turning them over halfway through the cooking time.

4. While the ribs are cooking, make the sauce. Combine the remaining sherry, blackberry preserves, hoisin sauce, garlic and ginger in a small saucepan. Bring to a simmer on the stovetop for a few minutes, until the sauce thickens.

5. When the time is up on the air fryer, turn the ribs over, pour a little sauce on the ribs and air-fry for another 10 minutes at 330°F. Turn the ribs over again, pour on more of the sauce and air-fry at 330°F for a final 10 minutes.

6. Let the ribs rest for at least 5 minutes before serving them warm with a little more glaze brushed on and the scallions and sesame seeds sprinkled on top.

Technique Tip

Putting some sherry in the bottom of the air fryer is a little trick that serves two functions. It helps prevent the oil that drains away from the ribs from smoking in the air fryer. It also helps to keep the ribs moist and flavorful. If you don't want to use sherry, you can substitute stock, wine or even some water.

Per Serving 620 Calories – 18g Fat (6g Sat. Fat) – 125mg Cholesterol – 55g Carbohydrates – 2g Fiber – 34g Sugar – 53g Protein

Sweet and Sour Pork

Serves: **2 to 4** ■ Temperature: **400˚F** ■ Cooking Time: **11 minutes**

¹/₃ cup all-purpose flour

¹/₃ cup cornstarch

2 teaspoons Chinese 5-spice powder

1 teaspoon salt

freshly ground black pepper

1 egg

2 tablespoons milk

¾ pound boneless pork,
cut into 1-inch cubes

vegetable or canola oil, in a spray bottle

1½ cups large chunks of
red and green peppers

½ cup ketchup

2 tablespoons rice wine vinegar
or apple cider vinegar

2 tablespoons brown sugar

¼ cup orange juice

1 tablespoon soy sauce

1 clove garlic, minced

1 cup cubed pineapple

chopped scallions

1. Set up a dredging station with two bowls. Combine the flour, cornstarch, Chinese 5-spice powder, salt and pepper in one large bowl. Whisk the egg and milk together in a second bowl. Dredge the pork cubes in the flour mixture first, then dip them into the egg and then back into the flour to coat on all sides. Spray the coated pork cubes with vegetable or canola oil.

2. Pre-heat the air fryer to 400°F.

3. Toss the pepper chunks with a little oil and air-fry at 400°F for 5 minutes, shaking the basket halfway through the cooking time.

4. While the peppers are cooking, start making the sauce. Combine the ketchup, rice wine vinegar, brown sugar, orange juice, soy sauce, and garlic in a medium saucepan and bring the mixture to a boil on the stovetop. Reduce the heat and simmer for 5 minutes. When the peppers have finished air-frying, add them to the saucepan along with the pineapple chunks. Simmer the peppers and pineapple in the sauce for an additional 2 minutes. Set aside and keep warm.

5. Add the dredged pork cubes to the air fryer basket and air-fry at 400°F for 6 minutes, shaking the basket to turn the cubes over for the last minute of the cooking process.

6. When ready to serve, toss the cooked pork with the pineapple, peppers and sauce. Serve over white rice and garnish with chopped scallions.

Substitution Tip
This sweet and sour sauce is a good one to have under your belt. You can swap out the pork for chicken or tofu and it works just as well.

Per Serving 290 Calories – 10g Fat (2.5g Sat. Fat) – 55mg Cholesterol – 30g Carbohydrates – 2g Fiber – 23g Sugar – 21g Protein

Lollipop Lamb Chops with Mint Pesto

Serves: **4** ■ Temperature: **400˚F** ■ Cooking Time: **7 minutes**

Easy

GF

Mint Pesto

½ small clove garlic

¼ cup packed fresh parsley

¾ cup packed fresh mint

½ teaspoon lemon juice

¼ cup grated Parmesan cheese

⅓ cup shelled pistachios

¼ teaspoon salt

½ cup olive oil

8 "frenched" lamb chops (1 rack)

olive oil

salt and freshly ground black pepper

1 tablespoon dried rosemary, chopped

1 tablespoon dried thyme

1. Make the pesto by combining the garlic, parsley and mint in a food processor and process until finely chopped. Add the lemon juice, Parmesan cheese, pistachios and salt. Process until all the ingredients have turned into a paste. With the processor running, slowly pour the olive oil in through the feed tube. Scrape the sides of the processor with a spatula and process for another 30 seconds.

2. Pre-heat the air fryer to 400°F.

3. Rub both sides of the lamb chops with olive oil and season with salt, pepper, rosemary and thyme, pressing the herbs into the meat gently with your fingers. Transfer the lamb chops to the air fryer basket.

4. Air-fry the lamb chops at 400°F for 5 minutes. Flip the chops over and air-fry for an additional 2 minutes. This should bring the chops to a medium-rare doneness, depending on their thickness. Adjust the cooking time up or down a minute or two accordingly for different degrees of doneness.

5. Serve the lamb chops with mint pesto drizzled on top.

Did You Know?

A "frenched" rack of lamb is one with the bones exposed. You can find a "frenched" rack of lamb in most grocery stores, or you can ask your butcher to "french" the rack for you. Once you have the rack of lamb home, simply cut the rack into chops by cutting in between the bones. Et voilà – lollipop lamb chops!

Per Serving
Lamb Chops without Pesto 680 Calories – 63g Fat (27g Sat. Fat) – 130mg Cholesterol – 1g Carbohydrates – 1g Fiber – 0g Sugar – 25g Protein
Pesto 330 Calories – 34g Fat (5g Sat. Fat) – 5mg Cholesterol – 5g Carbohydrates – 2g Fiber – 1g Sugar – 5g Protein

Lamb Meatballs with Quick Tomato Sauce

Serves: **4 (20 meatballs)** ■ Temperature: **400˚F** ■ Cooking Time: **8 minutes**

½ small onion, finely diced

1 clove garlic, minced

1 pound ground lamb

2 tablespoons fresh parsley, finely chopped (plus more for garnish)

2 teaspoons fresh oregano, finely chopped

2 tablespoons milk

1 egg yolk

salt and freshly ground black pepper

½ cup crumbled feta cheese, for garnish

Tomato Sauce:

2 tablespoons butter

1 clove garlic, smashed

pinch crushed red pepper flakes

¼ teaspoon ground cinnamon

1 (28-ounce) can crushed tomatoes

salt, to taste

Easy

GF

1. Combine all ingredients for the meatballs in a large bowl and mix just until everything is combined. Shape the mixture into 1½-inch balls or shape the meat between two spoons to make quenelles (little three-sided footballs).

2. Pre-heat the air fryer to 400°F.

3. While the air fryer is pre-heating, start the quick tomato sauce. Place the butter, garlic and red pepper flakes in a sauté pan and heat over medium heat on the stovetop. Let the garlic sizzle a little, but before the butter starts to brown, add the cinnamon and tomatoes. Bring to a simmer and simmer for 15 minutes. Season to taste with salt (but not too much as the feta that you will be sprinkling on at the end will be salty).

4. Brush the bottom of the air fryer basket with a little oil and transfer the meatballs to the air fryer basket in one layer, air-frying in batches if necessary.

5. Air-fry at 400°F for 8 minutes, giving the basket a shake once during the cooking process to turn the meatballs over.

6. To serve, spoon a pool of the tomato sauce onto plates and add the meatballs in a decorative manner. Sprinkle the feta cheese on top and garnish with more fresh parsley. Serve with rice or orzo pasta, or just a simple Greek salad.

Serving Suggestion

I love pairing lamb with cinnamon (in the tomato sauce) and the feta offers a nice salty contrast that cuts through the rich lamb flavor. You could even make this an appetizer instead of an entrée if you like, serving with toothpicks.

Per Serving
Lamb Meatballs without Tomato Sauce 400 Calories – 32g Fat (15g Sat. Fat) – 145mg Cholesterol – 4g Carbohydrates – 1g Fiber – 2g Sugar – 23g Protein
Quick Tomato Sauce 340 Calories – 24g Fat (15g Sat. Fat) – 60mg Cholesterol – 33g Carbohydrates – 8g Fiber – 19g Sugar – 7g Protein

Chicken & Poultry

Sesame Orange Chicken

Serves: **2 to 3** ■ Temperature: **400˚F** ■ Cooking Time: **9 minutes**

1 pound boneless, skinless chicken breasts, cut into cubes

salt and freshly ground black pepper

¼ cup cornstarch

2 eggs, beaten

1½ cups panko breadcrumbs

vegetable or peanut oil, in a spray bottle

12 ounces orange marmalade

1 tablespoon soy sauce

1 teaspoon minced ginger

2 tablespoons hoisin sauce

1 tablespoon sesame oil

sesame seeds, toasted

1. Season the chicken pieces with salt and pepper. Set up a dredging station. Put the cornstarch in a zipper-sealable plastic bag. Place the beaten eggs in a bowl and put the panko breadcrumbs in a shallow dish. Transfer the seasoned chicken to the bag with the cornstarch and shake well to completely coat the chicken on all sides. Remove the chicken from the bag, shaking off any excess cornstarch and dip the pieces into the egg. Let any excess egg drip from the chicken and transfer into the breadcrumbs, pressing the crumbs onto the chicken pieces with your hands. Spray the chicken pieces with vegetable or peanut oil.

2. Pre-heat the air fryer to 400°F.

3. Combine the orange marmalade, soy sauce, ginger, hoisin sauce and sesame oil in a saucepan. Bring the mixture to a boil on the stovetop, lower the heat and simmer for 10 minutes, until the sauce has thickened. Set aside and keep warm.

4. Transfer the coated chicken to the air fryer basket and air-fry at 400°F for 9 minutes, shaking the basket a few times during the cooking process to help the chicken cook evenly.

5. Right before serving, toss the browned chicken pieces with the sesame orange sauce. Serve over white rice with steamed broccoli. Sprinkle the sesame seeds on top.

Prep Help

If you're making this for more than 3 people, multiply the recipe accordingly and cook the chicken in batches. When all the chicken is cooked, return it all to the air fryer and air-fry at 350°F for 3 to 4 minutes to reheat. Then toss everything with the warm sauce and serve.

Per Serving 700 Calories – 16g Fat (3g Sat. Fat) – 190mg Cholesterol – 95g Carbohydrates – 3g Fiber – 72g Sugar – 51g Protein

Parmesan Crusted Chicken Cordon Bleu

Serves: **2** ■ Temperature: **350˚F** ■ Cooking Time: **14 minutes**

GF*

2 (6-ounce) boneless, skinless chicken breasts

salt and freshly ground black pepper

1 tablespoon Dijon mustard

4 slices Swiss cheese

4 slices deli-sliced ham

¼ cup all-purpose flour*

1 egg, beaten

¾ cup panko breadcrumbs*

⅓ cup grated Parmesan cheese

olive oil, in a spray bottle

*Make this recipe gluten free by using gluten-free flour and gluten-free panko breadcrumbs.

1. Butterfly the chicken breasts. Place the chicken breast on a cutting board and press down on the breast with the palm of your hand. Slice into the long side of the chicken breast, parallel to the cutting board, but not all the way through to the other side. Open the chicken breast like a "book". Place a piece of plastic wrap over the chicken breast and gently pound it with a meat mallet to make it evenly thick.

2. Season the chicken with salt and pepper. Spread the Dijon mustard on the inside of each chicken breast. Layer one slice of cheese on top of the mustard, then top with the 2 slices of ham and the other slice of cheese.

3. Starting with the long edge of the chicken breast, roll the chicken up to the other side. Secure it shut with 1 or 2 toothpicks.

4. Pre-heat the air fryer to 350°F.

5. Set up a dredging station with three shallow dishes. Place the flour in the first dish. Place the beaten egg in the second shallow dish. Combine the panko breadcrumbs and Parmesan cheese together in the third shallow dish. Dip the stuffed and rolled chicken breasts in the flour, then the beaten egg and then roll in the breadcrumb-cheese mixture to cover on all sides. Press the crumbs onto the chicken breasts with your hands to make sure they are well adhered. Spray the chicken breasts with olive oil and transfer to the air fryer basket.

6. Air-fry at 350°F for 14 minutes, flipping the breasts over halfway through the cooking time. Let the chicken rest for a few minutes before removing the toothpicks, slicing and serving.

Dress It Up

If you'd like to dress up this chicken dish for a dinner party, here is a simple but delicious sauce that you can make while the chicken is cooking. Slice the chicken diagonally, fan it out on the plate, top it with this sauce and you'll be the star of the evening.

Per Serving
Parmesan Crusted Chicken Cordon Bleu   600 Calories – 24g Fat (13g Sat. Fat) – 280mg Cholesterol – 13g Carbohydrates – 1g Fiber – 2g Sugar – 83g Protein
Brandy Mustard Cream Sauce   310 Calories – 21g Fat (12g Sat. Fat) – 60mg Cholesterol – 7g Carbohydrates – 1g Fiber – 3g Sugar – 4g Protein

Brandy Mustard Cream Sauce

1 teaspoon olive oil

1 shallot, minced

¼ cup brandy

1 cup chicken stock

1 tablespoon Dijon mustard

¼ cup heavy cream

1 tablespoon butter

1 teaspoon fresh thyme leaves

salt and freshly ground black pepper

1. Pre-heat a medium saucepan over medium-high heat. Add the olive oil and sauté the shallot until brown – about 2 minutes. Deglaze the pan by adding the brandy and scraping up any bits of brown on the bottom of the pan. Simmer and reduce the volume of the brandy by half.

2. Add the chicken stock, Dijon mustard and heavy cream and whisk until smooth. Simmer gently until the sauce has thickened – about 8 minutes. (If you'd like a super smooth sauce, strain the mixture through a fine strainer to remove the shallots. Otherwise, just continue with the recipe.)

3. Remove the pan from the heat, add the butter and fresh thyme and swirl until the butter has melted. Season with salt and pepper to taste and serve.

How to Bread and Dredge

Primer

So many fried foods are not just simply fried, but breaded and fried and it's the breading that is so important to the flavor and texture of the finished food. As a result, the breading process is pretty important. You want to make sure your breading is full of flavor and you want to make sure your breading stays put and doesn't fall off the food. Here's how you can achieve both of those goals.

■ **Use the proper breading technique.** There are usually three steps to breading foods and they are all important. Don't skip a step! Coat foods with flour first, then egg and then the breadcrumbs. It may feel counter-intuitive to start with the flour, but the flour works as the glue between the food and the egg. It's the flour that will bind the two together and keep your breading where you want it to be – on the food, not on the bottom of the air fryer. The egg (or buttermilk) will work as the glue between the flour and the crumbs. The crumbs will give you the final flavor and texture. Be diligent about the breadcrumbs and press them onto the food with your hands. Because the air fryer has a powerful fan as part of its mechanism, breading can sometimes blow off the food. Pressing those crumbs on firmly will help the breading adhere.

■ **Season your stages.** In most cases, you should season both the flour and the breadcrumb stages of your breading process. The only chance the food itself gets seasoned is if you season the flour with salt and pepper (or season the food before dredging it in the flour). In order for the breading to be properly seasoned, however, you should also season the breadcrumbs. The exception to this rule is when there is an ingredient in the mix that is inherently salty, like Parmesan cheese.

■ **Chill out.** While it's not completely necessary, chilling your breaded foods in the refrigerator for 10 to 15 minutes before air-frying will give the breading time to adhere to the food better.

■ **Spritz with oil.** You will still need oil on the breading in order to get it to brown nicely. Oil will not only help brown the food, but also helps to keep the breadcrumbs or flour coating moist and prevents them from drying out. In deep-frying, oil plays a big role in cooking the food, browning and keeping it moist. We still need the oil in air-frying, but we can get away with using a whole lot less.

■ **Breadcrumbs.** There are a lot of different types of breadcrumbs used in this cookbook.

● **Panko breadcrumbs** are made from a crust-less white bread (although you can find a tan variety that is made with crusts as well) and are lighter, flakier and crispier than regular breadcrumbs. Because they resist absorbing oils, they will give you a crispier finish.

● **Plain or fresh breadcrumbs** are made from fresh bread and are finer than panko breadcrumbs. They produce a softer coating or crust on foods.

● **Toasted or dried breadcrumbs** are made from bread that has been previously toasted and consequently will give you a crispier coating than fresh breadcrumbs, but not as crispy as panko breadcrumbs.

● **Seasoned breadcrumbs** can be purchased from stores and are breadcrumbs with Italian dried herbs mixed in.

● **Make your own.** You can make your own version of fresh, dried or seasoned breadcrumbs and they will probably taste better than a store-bought variety. Use a food processor or blender to process fresh bread to the right consistency to make fresh breadcrumbs, process toasted bread to make toasted or dried breadcrumbs, and process toasted bread along with some Italian dried herbs (like oregano and thyme) to make seasoned breadcrumbs.

■ **Gluten-Free Substitutions.** Many people are looking for gluten-free substitutions these days and those searching to replicate fried foods will be relieved to know that there is a way!

● Here are some gluten-free substitutions for flour, although you might experience a slight difference in flavor.

◆ Gluten-free flour
◆ Chickpea flour
◆ Rice flour (brown and white)
◆ Potato Flour
◆ Almond flour (or other nut flours)
◆ Spelt flour
◆ Millet flour
◆ Coconut flour
◆ Corn flour
◆ Cornstarch

● Here are some gluten-free substitutions for breadcrumbs:

◆ Gluten-free breadcrumbs
◆ Gluten-free panko breadcrumbs
◆ Gluten-free crackers, ground in a food processor
◆ Corn tortilla chips, ground in a food processor
◆ Cornmeal
◆ Ground nuts

Nashville Hot Chicken

Serves: 4 ■ Temperature: 370°F + 340°F ■ Cooking Time: 20 minutes per batch + 7 minutes

Easy

1 (4-pound) chicken, cut into 6 pieces
(2 breasts, 2 thighs and 2 drumsticks)

2 eggs

1 cup buttermilk

2 cups all-purpose flour

2 tablespoons paprika

1 teaspoon garlic powder

1 teaspoon onion powder

2 teaspoons salt

1 teaspoon freshly ground black pepper

vegetable oil, in a spray bottle

Nashville Hot Sauce:

1 tablespoon cayenne pepper

1 teaspoon salt

¼ cup vegetable oil

4 slices white bread

dill pickle slices

1. Cut the chicken breasts into 2 pieces so that you have a total of 8 pieces of chicken.

2. Set up a two-stage dredging station. Whisk the eggs and buttermilk together in a bowl. Combine the flour, paprika, garlic powder, onion powder, salt and black pepper in a zipper-sealable plastic bag. Dip the chicken pieces into the egg-buttermilk mixture, then toss them in the seasoned flour, coating all sides. Repeat this procedure (egg mixture and then flour mixture) one more time. This can be a little messy, but make sure all sides of the chicken are completely covered. Spray the chicken with vegetable oil and set aside.

3. Pre-heat the air fryer to 370°F. Spray or brush the bottom of the air-fryer basket with a little vegetable oil.

4. Air-fry the chicken in two batches at 370°F for 20 minutes, flipping the pieces over halfway through the cooking process. Transfer the chicken to a plate, but do not cover. Repeat with the second batch of chicken.

5. Lower the temperature on the air fryer to 340°F. Flip the chicken back over and place the first batch of chicken on top of the second batch already in the basket. Air-fry for another 7 minutes.

6. While the chicken is air-frying, combine the cayenne pepper and salt in a bowl. Heat the vegetable oil in a small saucepan and when it is very hot, add it to the spice mix, whisking until smooth. It will sizzle briefly when you add it to the spices. Place the fried chicken on top of the white bread slices and brush the hot sauce all over chicken. Top with the pickle slices and serve warm. Enjoy the heat and the flavor!

One of Meredith's Favorites

One of my favorite recipes in this book, Nashville Hot Chicken, is also known as "the Bird that Bites Back". It's the hot sauce slathered on at the end that bites, so go easy if you don't want it too spicy! Traditionally hot chicken is served on slices of white bread to absorb the juice, and then topped with cool dill pickle slices. If you need more help with the heat, here is a cool lemon-dill dressing that you can use as a dip or pour right on top.

Lemon-Dill Buttermilk Dressing

½ cup buttermilk

½ cup sour cream or Greek yogurt

salt and freshly ground black pepper, to taste

½ teaspoon lemon zest

1 teaspoon lemon juice

1 tablespoon fresh chopped dill

1. Combine all ingredients in a bowl.

Per Serving
Nashville Hot Chicken   670 Calories – 27g Fat (7g Sat. Fat) – 260mg Cholesterol –
13g Carbohydrates – 1g Fiber – 1g Sugar – 89gProtein

Lemon-Dill Buttermilk Dressing   35 Calories – 1g Fat (0.5g Sat. Fat) – 5mg Cholesterol –
3g Carbohydrates – 0g Fiber – 2g Sugar – 4g Protein

Teriyaki Chicken Drumsticks

Serves: **2** ■ Temperature: **380˚F** ■ Cooking Time: **17 minutes**

2 tablespoons soy sauce*

¼ cup dry sherry

1 tablespoon brown sugar

2 tablespoons water

1 tablespoon rice wine vinegar

1 clove garlic, crushed

1-inch fresh ginger, peeled and sliced

pinch crushed red pepper flakes

4 to 6 bone-in, skin-on
chicken drumsticks

1 tablespoon cornstarch

fresh cilantro leaves

*Make this recipe gluten free by using
a gluten-free soy sauce.

1. Make the marinade by combining the soy sauce, dry sherry, brown sugar, water, rice vinegar, garlic, ginger and crushed red pepper flakes. Pour the marinade over the chicken legs, cover and let the chicken marinate for 1 to 4 hours in the refrigerator.

2. Pre-heat the air fryer to 380°F.

3. Transfer the chicken from the marinade to the air fryer basket, transferring any extra marinade to a small saucepan. Air-fry at 380°F for 8 minutes. Flip the chicken over and continue to air-fry for another 6 minutes, watching to make sure it doesn't brown too much.

4. While the chicken is cooking, bring the reserved marinade to a simmer on the stovetop. Dissolve the cornstarch in 2 tablespoons of water and stir this into the saucepan. Bring to a boil to thicken the sauce. Remove the garlic clove and slices of ginger from the sauce and set aside.

5. When the time is up on the air fryer, brush the thickened sauce on the chicken and air-fry for 3 more minutes. Remove the chicken from the air fryer and brush with the remaining sauce.

6. Serve over rice and sprinkle the cilantro leaves on top.

Substitution Tip

You can easily swap bone-in chicken breasts for the chicken legs in this recipe. The timing should be about the same, unless the chicken breasts you have are huge. If that's the case, increase the cooking time a little, but watch the chicken so that it doesn't over-brown. You can also cheat a little and buy a bottle of teriyaki sauce instead of making your own marinade. I won't tell anyone! Just make sure you bring the marinade to a boil before brushing it on the finished chicken.

Per Serving 370 Calories – 16g Fat (4.5g Sat. Fat) – 205mg Cholesterol –
14g Carbohydrates – 0g Fiber – 9g Sugar – 38g Protein

Maple Bacon Wrapped Chicken Breasts

Serves: **2** ■ Temperature: **380˚F** ■ Cooking Time: **18 minutes**

2 (6-ounce) boneless, skinless chicken breasts

2 tablespoons maple syrup, divided

freshly ground black pepper

6 slices thick-sliced bacon

fresh celery or parsley leaves

Ranch Dressing:

¼ cup mayonnaise

¼ cup buttermilk

¼ cup Greek yogurt

1 tablespoon chopped fresh chives

1 tablespoon chopped fresh parsley

1 tablespoon chopped fresh dill

1 tablespoon lemon juice

salt and freshly ground black pepper

1. Brush the chicken breasts with half the maple syrup and season with freshly ground black pepper. Wrap three slices of bacon around each chicken breast, securing the ends with toothpicks.

2. Pre-heat the air fryer to 380°F.

3. Air-fry the chicken for 6 minutes. Then turn the chicken breasts over, pour more maple syrup on top and air-fry for another 6 minutes. Turn the chicken breasts one more time, brush the remaining maple syrup all over and continue to air-fry for a final 6 minutes.

4. While the chicken is cooking, prepare the dressing by combining all the dressing ingredients together in a bowl.

5. When the chicken has finished cooking, remove the toothpicks and serve each breast with a little dressing drizzled over each one. Scatter lots of fresh celery or parsley leaves on top.

Easy

GF

Note from Meredith
This recipe reminds me of a chicken club sandwich, but without the bread! You can use regular bacon for this recipe, but thick-sliced bacon is easier to pin to the chicken breasts with toothpicks.

Per Serving
Maple Bacon Chicken Breast 450 Calories – 16g Fat (5g Sat. Fat) – 205mg Cholesterol – 16g Carbohydrates – 1g Fiber – 14g Sugar - 62g Protein
Ranch Dressing 210 Calories – 22g Fat (4g Sat. Fat) – 15mg Cholesterol – 2g Carbohydrates – 0g Fiber – 2g Sugar – 1g Protein

Crispy Fried Onion Chicken Breasts

Serves: **2** ■ Temperature: **380˚F** ■ Cooking Time: **13 minutes**

¼ cup all-purpose flour*

salt and freshly ground black pepper

1 egg

2 tablespoons Dijon mustard

1½ cups crispy fried onions (like French's®)

½ teaspoon paprika

2 (5-ounce) boneless, skinless chicken breasts

vegetable or olive oil, in a spray bottle

*Make this recipe gluten free by using gluten-free flour.

1. Pre-heat the air fryer to 380°F.

2. Set up a dredging station with three shallow dishes. Place the flour in the first shallow dish and season well with salt and freshly ground black pepper. Combine the egg and Dijon mustard in a second shallow dish and whisk until smooth. Place the fried onions in a sealed bag and using a rolling pin, crush them into coarse crumbs. Combine these crumbs with the paprika in the third shallow dish.

3. Dredge the chicken breasts in the flour. Shake off any excess flour and dip them into the egg mixture. Let any excess egg drip off. Then coat both sides of the chicken breasts with the crispy onions. Press the crumbs onto the chicken breasts with your hands to make sure they are well adhered.

4. Spray or brush the bottom of the air fryer basket with oil. Transfer the chicken breasts to the air fryer basket and air-fry at 380°F for 13 minutes, turning the chicken over halfway through the cooking time.

5. Serve immediately.

Easy
GF*

Serving Suggestion
This chicken would also make a delicious fried chicken sandwich with some coleslaw on top!

Per Serving 300 Calories – 11g Fat (4g Sat. Fat) – 170mg Cholesterol – 9g Carbohydrates – 0g Fiber – 0g Sugar – 45g Protein

Coconut Curry Chicken with Coconut Rice

Serves: 4 ■ Temperature: 380°F ■ Cooking Time: 24 + 27 + 5 minutes

GF

1 (14-ounce) can coconut milk

2 tablespoons green or red curry paste

zest and juice of one lime

1 clove garlic, minced

1 tablespoon grated fresh ginger

1 teaspoon ground cumin

1 (3- to 4-pound) chicken,
cut into 8 pieces

vegetable or olive oil

salt and freshly ground black pepper

fresh cilantro leaves

For the rice:

1 cup basmati or jasmine rice

1 cup water

1 cup coconut milk

½ teaspoon salt

freshly ground black pepper

1. Make the marinade by combining the coconut milk, curry paste, lime zest and juice, garlic, ginger and cumin. Coat the chicken on all sides with the marinade and marinate the chicken for 1 hour to overnight in the refrigerator.

2. Pre-heat the air fryer to 380°F.

3. Brush the bottom of the air fryer basket with oil. Transfer the chicken thighs and drumsticks from the marinade to the air fryer basket, letting most of the marinade drip off. Season to taste with salt and freshly ground black pepper.

4. Air-fry the chicken drumsticks and thighs at 380°F for 12 minutes. Flip the chicken over and continue to air-fry for another 12 minutes. Set aside and air-fry the chicken breast pieces at 380°F for 15 minutes. Turn the chicken breast pieces over and air-fry for another 12 minutes. Return the chicken thighs and drumsticks to the air fryer and air-fry for an additional 5 minutes.

5. While the chicken is cooking, make the coconut rice. Rinse the rice kernels with water and drain well. Place the rice in a medium saucepan with a tight fitting lid, along with the water, coconut milk, salt and freshly ground black pepper. Bring the mixture to a boil and then cover, reduce the heat and let it cook gently for 20 minutes without lifting the lid. When the time is up, lift the lid, fluff with a fork and set aside.

6. Remove the chicken from the air fryer and serve warm with the coconut rice and fresh cilantro scattered around.

Note from Meredith

This marinade gives the chicken a *subtle* curry and coconut flavor – not like a bold saucy curried chicken stew – and it helps the chicken brown beautifully while staying moist and tender inside. If you want more coconut flavor in the rice, toss the finished rice with a little coconut cream (the thick white cream that rises to the top of the can of coconut milk) at the end.

Per Serving 760 Calories - 22g Fat (11g Sat. Fat) – 250mg Cholesterol –
38g Carbohydrates - 0g Fiber – 1g Sugar · 95g Protein

Simple Buttermilk Fried Chicken

Serves: **4** ■ Temperature: **370°F + 340°F** ■ Cooking Time: **20 minutes per batch + 7 minutes**

Easy

GF*

1 (4-pound) chicken, cut into 8 pieces

2 cups buttermilk

hot sauce (optional)

1½ cups flour*

2 teaspoons paprika

1 teaspoon salt

freshly ground black pepper

2 eggs, lightly beaten

vegetable oil, in a spray bottle

*Make this recipe gluten free by using gluten-free flour.

1. Cut the chicken into 8 pieces and submerge them in the buttermilk and hot sauce, if using. A zipper-sealable plastic bag works well for this. Let the chicken soak in the buttermilk for at least one hour or even overnight in the refrigerator.

2. Set up a dredging station. Mix the flour, paprika, salt and black pepper in a clean zipper-sealable plastic bag. Whisk the eggs and place them in a shallow dish. Remove four pieces of chicken from the buttermilk and transfer them to the bag with the flour. Shake them around to coat on all sides. Remove the chicken from the flour, shaking off any excess flour, and dip them into the beaten egg. Return the chicken to the bag of seasoned flour and shake again. Set the coated chicken aside and repeat with the remaining four pieces of chicken.

3. Pre-heat the air fryer to 370°F.

4. Spray the chicken on all sides with the vegetable oil and then transfer one batch to the air fryer basket. Air-fry the chicken at 370°F for 20 minutes, flipping the pieces over halfway through the cooking process, taking care not to knock off the breading. Transfer the chicken to a plate, but do not cover. Repeat with the second batch of chicken.

5. Lower the temperature on the air fryer to 340°F. Flip the chicken back over and place the first batch of chicken on top of the second batch already in the basket. Air-fry for another 7 minutes and serve warm.

Serving Suggestion
Few things go better with fried chicken than coleslaw. Here's an easy recipe to help make your meal complete!

Per Serving
Buttermilk Fried Chicken 640 Calories – 24g Fat (7g Sat. Fat) – 265mg Cholesterol – 10g Carbohydrates – 0g Fiber – 0g Sugar – 89g Protein
Coleslaw 340 Calories – 28g Fat (4g Sat. Fat) – 0mg Cholesterol –22g Carbohydrates – 4g Fiber – 15g Sugar – 2g Protein

Coleslaw

3 cups shredded green cabbage
2 cups shredded red cabbage
½ cup thinly sliced white or red onion
(about ¼ onion), rinsed with water
½ teaspoon salt
1 cup shredded carrots
Vinaigrette:
½ cup white wine vinegar
3 tablespoons sugar
1 teaspoon mustard powder
1 tablespoon celery seed
½ cup vegetable oil
salt and freshly ground black pepper

1. Combine the cabbages and onion in a large bowl and toss with salt. Let the vegetables sit while you prepare the rest of the ingredients. Before dressing the cabbage, drain away any liquid that has accumulated in the bottom of the bowl and add the shredded carrots.

2. In a small saucepan, bring the vinegar, sugar, mustard powder and celery seed to a boil. Stir to dissolve the sugar. Remove the saucepan from the heat and whisk in the vegetable oil. Pour the hot vinaigrette over the cabbage and onions and toss well. Season to taste with salt and pepper. Cover and refrigerate until you are ready to serve.

Chicken Cutlets with Broccoli Rabe and Roasted Peppers

Serves: 2 ■ Temperature: 400°F + 360°F ■ Cooking Time: 10 minutes

½ bunch broccoli rabe

olive oil, in a spray bottle

salt and freshly ground black pepper

⅔ cup roasted red pepper strips

2 (4-ounce) boneless, skinless chicken breasts

2 tablespoons all-purpose flour*

1 egg, beaten

⅓ cup seasoned breadcrumbs*

2 slices aged provolone cheese

*Make this recipe gluten free by using gluten-free flour and gluten-free breadcrumbs.

1. Bring a medium saucepot of salted water to a boil on the stovetop. Blanch the broccoli rabe for 3 minutes in the boiling water and then drain. When it has cooled a little, squeeze out as much water as possible, drizzle a little olive oil on top, season with salt and black pepper and set aside. Dry the roasted red peppers with a clean kitchen towel and set them aside as well.

2. Place each chicken breast between 2 pieces of plastic wrap. Use a meat pounder to flatten the chicken breasts to about ½-inch thick. Season the chicken on both sides with salt and pepper.

3. Preheat the air fryer to 400°F.

4. Set up a dredging station with three shallow dishes. Place the flour in one dish, the egg in a second dish and the breadcrumbs in a third dish. Coat the chicken on all sides with the flour. Shake off any excess flour and dip the chicken into the egg. Let the excess egg drip off and coat both sides of the chicken in the breadcrumbs. Spray the chicken with olive oil on both sides and transfer to the air fryer basket.

5. Air-fry the chicken at 400°F for 5 minutes. Turn the chicken over and air-fry for another minute. Then, top the chicken breast with the broccoli rabe and roasted peppers. Place a slice of the provolone cheese on top and secure it with a toothpick or two.

6. Air-fry at 360° for 3 to 4 minutes to melt the cheese and warm everything together.

Did You Know?

Broccoli rabe is used a lot in Southern Italian cuisine. It is a nutty and somewhat bitter leafy green vegetable and gives this dish a unique flavor, especially when teamed up with the aged provolone. Broccoli rabe needs to be blanched for a few minutes to remove some of its bitterness. This dish also makes a great sandwich – slice the chicken breast in half and serve on a long crusty hoagie or torpedo roll.

Per Serving 440 Calories –16g Fat (7g Sat. Fat) – 165mg Cholesterol – 21g Carbohydrates – 6g Fiber – 2g Sugar - 50g Protein

Spicy Black Bean Turkey Burgers with Cumin-Avocado Spread

Serves: **2** ■ Temperature: **380˚F** ■ Cooking Time: **20 minutes**

Easy

1 cup canned black beans, drained and rinsed

¾ pound lean ground turkey

2 tablespoons minced red onion

1 Jalapeño pepper, seeded and minced

2 tablespoons plain breadcrumbs

½ teaspoon chili powder

¼ teaspoon cayenne pepper

salt, to taste

olive or vegetable oil

2 slices pepper jack cheese

toasted burger rolls, sliced tomatoes, lettuce leaves

Cumin-Avocado Spread:

1 ripe avocado

juice of 1 lime

1 teaspoon ground cumin

½ teaspoon salt

1 tablespoon chopped fresh cilantro

freshly ground black pepper

1. Place the black beans in a large bowl and smash them slightly with the back of a fork. Add the ground turkey, red onion, Jalapeño pepper, breadcrumbs, chili powder and cayenne pepper. Season with salt. Mix with your hands to combine all the ingredients and then shape them into 2 patties. Brush both sides of the burger patties with a little olive or vegetable oil.

2. Pre-heat the air fryer to 380°F.

3. Transfer the burgers to the air fryer basket and air-fry for 20 minutes, flipping them over halfway through the cooking process. Top the burgers with the pepper jack cheese (securing the slices to the burgers with a toothpick) for the last 2 minutes of the cooking process.

4. While the burgers are cooking, make the cumin avocado spread. Place the avocado, lime juice, cumin and salt in food processor and process until smooth. (For a chunkier spread, you can mash this by hand in a bowl.) Stir in the cilantro and season with freshly ground black pepper. Chill the spread until you are ready to serve.

5. When the burgers have finished cooking, remove them from the air fryer and let them rest on a plate, covered gently with aluminum foil. Brush a little olive oil on the insides of the burger rolls. Place the rolls, cut side up, into the air fryer basket and air-fry at 400°F for 1 minute to toast and warm them.

6. Spread the cumin-avocado spread on the rolls and build your burgers with lettuce and sliced tomatoes and any other ingredient you like. Serve warm with a side of sweet potato fries.

Keep It Cool

These burgers do have a little kick to them. If you're not one for spicy foods, just eliminate the Jalapeño pepper and cayenne from the burger mix and pick a Cheddar or Swiss cheese to melt on top.

Per Serving 570 Calories – 11g Fat (3g Sat. Fat) – 150mg Cholesterol – 47g Carbohydrates – 10g Fiber – 7g Sugar – 74g Protein

Lemon Sage Roast Chicken

Serves: **4** ■ Temperature: **350°F** ■ Cooking Time: **60 minutes**

Easy

GF

1 (4-pound) chicken

1 bunch sage, divided

1 lemon, zest and juice

salt and freshly ground black pepper

1. Pre-heat the air fryer to 350°F and pour a little water into the bottom of the air fryer drawer. (This will help prevent the grease that drips into the bottom drawer from burning and smoking.)

2. Run your fingers between the skin and flesh of the chicken breasts and thighs. Push a couple of sage leaves up underneath the skin of the chicken on each breast and each thigh.

3. Push some of the lemon zest up under the skin of the chicken next to the sage. Sprinkle some of the zest inside the chicken cavity, and reserve any leftover zest. Squeeze the lemon juice all over the chicken and in the cavity as well.

4. Season the chicken, inside and out, with the salt and freshly ground black pepper. Set a few sage leaves aside for the final garnish. Crumple up the remaining sage leaves and push them into the cavity of the chicken, along with one of the squeezed lemon halves.

5. Place the chicken breast side up into the air fryer basket and air-fry for 20 minutes at 350°F. Flip the chicken over so that it is breast side down and continue to air-fry for another 20 minutes. Return the chicken to breast side up and finish air-frying for 20 more minutes. The internal temperature of the chicken should register 165°F in the thickest part of the thigh when fully cooked. Remove the chicken from the air fryer and let it rest on a cutting board for at least 5 minutes.

6. Cut the rested chicken into pieces, sprinkle with the reserved lemon zest and garnish with the reserved sage leaves.

Prep Help
This recipe calls for a 4-pound chicken, which means you will need a larger air fryer (5-quarts or larger). To make this chicken dish in a 3-quart air fryer, cut the chicken into pieces – 2 breasts, 2 thighs and 2 drumsticks. Prepare the chicken the same way, pushing the sage leaves and lemon zest under the skin and seasoning all over with salt and lemon juice. Air-fry the chicken in two batches at 350°F for 12 minutes, flip the pieces over and air-fry for another 12 minutes. Warm the first batch of chicken by popping it on top of the second batch for the last 3 to 4 minutes of cooking time.

Per Serving 660 Calories – 27g Fat (6g Sat. Fat) – 245mg Cholesterol – 15g Carbohydrates – 14g Fiber – 0g Sugar - 87g Protein

Thai Turkey and Zucchini Meatballs

Serves: **4 to 6** ■ Temperature: **380°F** ■ Cooking Time: **10 to 12 minutes per batch**

1½ cups grated zucchini,
squeezed dry in a clean kitchen towel
(about 1 large zucchini)

3 scallions, finely chopped

2 cloves garlic, minced

1 tablespoon grated fresh ginger

1 tablespoon finely chopped fresh cilantro

zest of 1 lime

1 teaspoon salt

freshly ground black pepper

1½ pounds ground turkey
(a mix of light and dark meat)

2 eggs, lightly beaten

1 cup Thai sweet chili sauce
(spring roll sauce)

lime wedges, for serving

1.   Combine the zucchini, scallions, garlic, ginger, cilantro, lime zest, salt, pepper, ground turkey and eggs in a bowl and mix the ingredients together. Gently shape the mixture into 24 balls, about the size of golf balls.

2.   Pre-heat the air fryer to 380°F.

3.   Working in batches, air-fry the meatballs for 10 to 12 minutes, turning the meatballs over halfway through the cooking time. As soon as the meatballs have finished cooking, toss them in a bowl with the Thai sweet chili sauce to coat.

4.   Serve the meatballs over rice noodles or white rice with the remaining Thai sweet chili sauce and lime wedges to squeeze over the top.

GF

Serving Suggestion
These meatballs also make a tasty appetizer in a smaller size, served with toothpicks.

Per Serving
Thai Turkey Meatballs 330 Calories - 16g Fat (4.5g Sat. Fat) - 150mg Cholesterol - 25g Carbohydrates - 1g Fiber - 20g Sugar - 22g Protein

Air-Fried Turkey Breast with Cherry Glaze

Serves: **6 to 8** ■ Temperature: **350°F** ■ Cooking Time: **54 minutes**

1 (5-pound) turkey breast

2 teaspoons olive oil

1 teaspoon dried thyme

½ teaspoon dried sage

1 teaspoon salt

½ teaspoon freshly ground black pepper

½ cup cherry preserves

1 tablespoon chopped fresh thyme leaves

1 teaspoon soy sauce*

freshly ground black pepper

*Make this recipe gluten free by using a gluten-free soy sauce.

1. All turkeys are built differently, so depending on the turkey breast and how your butcher has prepared it, you may need to trim the bottom of the ribs in order to get the turkey to sit upright in the air fryer basket without touching the heating element. The key to this recipe is getting the right size turkey breast. Once you've managed that, the rest is easy, so make sure your turkey breast fits into the air fryer basket before you pre-heat the air fryer.

2. Pre-heat the air fryer to 350°F.

3. Brush the turkey breast all over with the olive oil. Combine the thyme, sage, salt and pepper and rub the outside of the turkey breast with the spice mixture.

4. Transfer the seasoned turkey breast to the air fryer basket, breast side up, and air-fry at 350°F for 25 minutes. Turn the turkey breast on its side and air-fry for another 12 minutes. Turn the turkey breast on the opposite side and air-fry for 12 more minutes. The internal temperature of the turkey breast should reach 165°F when fully cooked.

5. While the turkey is air-frying, make the glaze by combining the cherry preserves, fresh thyme, soy sauce and pepper in a small bowl. When the cooking time is up, return the turkey breast to an upright position and brush the glaze all over the turkey. Air-fry for a final 5 minutes, until the skin is nicely browned and crispy. Let the turkey rest, loosely tented with foil, for at least 5 minutes before slicing and serving.

GF*

Note from Meredith
You'll need a larger air fryer (5-quart air fryer or bigger) to make this recipe. If you have a 3-quart air fryer, you can cook a 3-pound bone-in split turkey breast. The timing will be very similar to the 5-pound bone-in full turkey breast because essentially you will have one 3-pound half breast alone, rather than two 2½-pound half breasts. Cut the seasonings and glaze ingredients in half. Cook for 20 minutes breast side up, then 20 minutes breast side down and finally another 15 minutes breast side up. Then, glaze the turkey and cook it for 5 more minutes.

Per Serving 430 Calories – 3g Fat (1g Sat. Fat) – 235mg Cholesterol – 10g Carbohydrates – 0g Fiber – 9g Sugar – 85g Protein

Fish & Seafood

Pecan-Orange Crusted Striped Bass

Serves: **2** ■ Temperature: **400°F** ■ Cooking Time: **8 to 9 minutes**

flour, for dredging*

2 egg whites, lightly beaten

1 cup pecans, chopped

1 teaspoon finely chopped orange zest, plus more for garnish

½ teaspoon salt

2 (6-ounce) fillets striped bass

salt and freshly ground black pepper

vegetable or olive oil, in a spray bottle

*Make this recipe gluten free by using a gluten-free flour.

Orange Cream Sauce (Optional)

½ cup fresh orange juice

¼ cup heavy cream

1 sprig fresh thyme

1. Set up a dredging station with three shallow dishes. Place the flour in one shallow dish. Place the beaten egg whites in a second shallow dish. Finally, combine the chopped pecans, orange zest and salt in a third shallow dish.

2. Coat the fish fillets one at a time. First season with salt and freshly ground black pepper. Then coat each fillet in flour. Shake off any excess flour and then dip the fish into the egg white. Let the excess egg drip off and then immediately press the fish into the pecan-orange mixture. Set the crusted fish fillets aside.

3. Pre-heat the air fryer to 400°F.

4. Spray the crusted fish with oil and then transfer the fillets to the air fryer basket. Air-fry for 8 to 9 minutes at 400°F, flipping the fish over halfway through the cooking time. The nuts on top should be nice and toasty and the fish should feel firm to the touch.

5. If you'd like to make a sauce to go with the fish while it cooks, combine the freshly squeezed orange juice, heavy cream and sprig of thyme in a small saucepan. Simmer on the stovetop for 5 minutes and then set aside.

6. Remove the fish from the air fryer and serve over a bed of salad, like the one below. Then add a sprinkling of orange zest and a spoonful of the orange cream sauce over the top if desired.

Arugula and Radicchio with Lemon Vinaigrette

1 tablespoon white wine vinegar

1 teaspoon finely minced shallot

1 teaspoon lemon zest

2 tablespoons freshly squeezed lemon juice

¼ cup extra virgin olive oil

½ teaspoon salt

freshly ground black pepper

2 ounces baby arugula (2 good handfuls)

¼ head of radicchio, thinly sliced

1. Make the vinaigrette by whisking together everything but the arugula and radicchio in a small bowl.

2. Toss the arugula and radicchio together and dress with the vinaigrette.

Per Serving
Pecan Crusted Striped Bass 430 Calories - 22g Fat (2.5g Sat. Fat) - 135mg Cholesterol - 24g Carbohydrates - 3g Fiber - 1g Sugar - 36g Protein

Orange Cream Sauce 130 Calories - 11g Fat (7g Sat. Fat) - 40mg Cholesterol - 7g Carbohydrates - 0g Fiber - 6g Sugar - 1g Protein

Arugula and Radicchio Salad 80 Calories - 7g Fat (1g Sat. Fat) - 0mg Cholesterol - 4g Carbohydrates - 1g Fiber - 1g Sugar - 1g Protein

Five Spice Red Snapper with Green Onions and Orange Salsa

Serves: **2** ■ Temperature: **400°F** ■ Cooking Time: **8 minutes**

Easy

GF

2 oranges, peeled, segmented and chopped

1 tablespoon minced shallot

1 to 3 teaspoons minced red Jalapeño or Serrano pepper

1 tablespoon chopped fresh cilantro

lime juice, to taste

salt, to taste

2 (5- to 6-ounce) red snapper fillets

½ teaspoon Chinese five spice powder

salt and freshly ground black pepper

vegetable or olive oil, in a spray bottle

4 green onions, cut into 2-inch lengths

1. Start by making the salsa. Cut the peel off the oranges, slicing around the oranges to expose the flesh. Segment the oranges by cutting in between the membranes of the orange. Chop the segments roughly and combine in a bowl with the shallot, Jalapeño or Serrano pepper, cilantro, lime juice and salt. Set the salsa aside.

2. Pre-heat the air fryer to 400°F.

3. Season the fish fillets with the five-spice powder, salt and freshly ground black pepper. Spray both sides of the fish fillets with oil. Toss the green onions with a little oil.

4. Transfer the fish to the air fryer basket and scatter the green onions around the fish. Air-fry at 400°F for 8 minutes.

5. Remove the fish from the air fryer, along with the fried green onions. Serve with white rice and a spoonful of the salsa on top.

Prep Help
The skin of red snapper is so pretty that it's a shame to take it off before you cook. If you choose to leave it on, slash the skin in a crosshatch pattern and cook the snapper skin side up so that it crisps up a little.

Per Serving 220 Calories – 4g Fat (0.5g Sat. Fat) – 65mg Cholesterol – 10g Carbohydrates – 2g Fiber – 7g Sugar – 36g Protein

Salmon Puttanesca en Papillotte with Zucchini

Serves: **2** ■ Temperature: **400°F** ■ Cooking Time: **5 + 12 minutes**

GF

1 small zucchini, sliced into ¼-inch thick half moons

1 teaspoon olive oil

salt and freshly ground black pepper

2 (5-ounce) salmon fillets

1 beefsteak tomato, chopped (about 1 cup)

1 tablespoon capers, rinsed

10 black olives, pitted and sliced

2 tablespoons dry vermouth or white wine

2 tablespoons butter

¼ cup chopped fresh basil, chopped

1. Pre-heat the air fryer to 400°F.

2. Toss the zucchini with the olive oil, salt and freshly ground black pepper. Transfer the zucchini into the air fryer basket and air-fry for 5 minutes, shaking the basket once or twice during the cooking process.

3. Cut out 2 large rectangles of parchment paper – about 13-inches by 15-inches each. Divide the air-fried zucchini between the two pieces of parchment paper, placing the vegetables in the center of each rectangle.

4. Place a fillet of salmon on each pile of zucchini. Season the fish very well with salt and pepper. Toss the tomato, capers, olives and vermouth (or white wine) together in a bowl. Divide the tomato mixture between the two fish packages, placing it on top of the fish fillets and pouring any juice out of the bowl onto the fish. Top each fillet with a tablespoon of butter.

5. Fold up each parchment square. Bring two edges together and fold them over a few times, leaving some space above the fish. Twist the open sides together and upwards so they can serve as handles for the packet, but don't let them extend beyond the top of the air fryer basket.

6. Place the two packages into the air fryer and air-fry at 400°F for 12 minutes. The packages should be puffed up and slightly browned when fully cooked. Once cooked, let the fish sit in the parchment for 2 minutes.

7. Serve the fish in the parchment paper, or if desired, remove the parchment paper before serving. Garnish with a little fresh basil.

Technique Tip

Cooking fish en papillote is a great way to cook fish in the air fryer AND make a sauce at the same time. You can do any type of fish this way. Don't worry about the paper catching on fire. Paper ignites at 451°F, which is hotter than the highest setting on the air fryer. It might brown a little from the butter, but it won't catch fire.

Per Serving 420 Calories – 29g Fat (8g Sat. Fat) – 100mg Cholesterol – 9g Carbohydrates – 2g Fiber – 4g Sugar – 30g Protein

Shrimp, Chorizo and Fingerling Potatoes

Serves: **4** ▪ Temperature: **380˚F** ▪ Cooking Time: **6 + 5 + 5 minutes**

Easy

GF

½ red onion, chopped into 1-inch chunks

8 fingerling potatoes, sliced into 1-inch slices or halved lengthwise

1 teaspoon olive oil

salt and freshly ground black pepper

8 ounces raw chorizo sausage, sliced into 1-inch chunks

16 raw large shrimp, peeled, deveined and tails removed

1 lime

¼ cup chopped fresh cilantro

chopped orange zest (optional)

1. Pre-heat the air fryer to 380°F.

2. Combine the red onion and potato chunks in a bowl and toss with the olive oil, salt and freshly ground black pepper.

3. Transfer the vegetables to the air fryer basket and air-fry for 6 minutes, shaking the basket a few times during the cooking process.

4. Add the chorizo chunks and continue to air-fry for another 5 minutes.

5. Add the shrimp, season with salt and continue to air-fry, shaking the basket every once in a while, for another 5 minutes.

6. Transfer the tossed shrimp, chorizo and potato to a bowl and squeeze some lime juice over the top to taste. Toss in the fresh cilantro, orange zest and a drizzle of olive oil, and season again to taste.

7. Serve with a fresh green salad.

Did You Know?

Chorizo sausage hails from Spain and its delicious paprika flavor and spicy kick makes it a favorite of mine. It pairs so nicely with shrimp, and the potatoes hold any flavor that tries to escape. This is an easy meal when paired with a side salad.

Per Serving 420 Calories – 24g Fat (9g Sat. Fat) – 170mg Cholesterol – 22g Carbohydrates – 3g Fiber – 2g Sugar – 29g Protein

Shrimp Sliders with Avocado

Serves: **4 to 8** ■ Temperature: **380°F** ■ Cooking Time: **10 minutes**

16 raw jumbo shrimp, peeled, deveined and tails removed (about 1 pound)

1 rib celery, finely chopped

2 carrots, grated (about ½ cup)

2 teaspoons lemon juice

2 teaspoons Dijon mustard

¼ cup chopped fresh basil or parsley

½ cup breadcrumbs

½ teaspoon salt

freshly ground black pepper

vegetable or olive oil, in a spray bottle

8 slider buns

mayonnaise

butter lettuce

2 avocados, sliced and peeled

1. Put the shrimp into a food processor and pulse it a few times to rough chop the shrimp. Remove three quarters of the shrimp and transfer it to a bowl. Continue to process the remaining shrimp in the food processor until it is a smooth purée. Transfer the purée to the bowl with the chopped shrimp.

2. Add the celery, carrots, lemon juice, mustard, basil, breadcrumbs, salt and pepper to the bowl and combine well.

3. Pre-heat the air fryer to 380°F.

4. While the air fryer pre-heats, shape the shrimp mixture into 8 patties. Spray both sides of the patties with oil and transfer one layer of patties to the air fryer basket. Air-fry for 10 minutes, flipping the patties over halfway through the cooking time.

5. Prepare the slider rolls by toasting them and spreading a little mayonnaise on both halves. Place a piece of butter lettuce on the bottom bun, top with the shrimp slider and then finish with the avocado slices on top. Pop the top half of the bun on top and enjoy!

Serving Suggestion
These little sliders are a fun main meal served with a side salad or some air-fried French fries, but they also make great appetizers and finger food. For a delicious alternative to the avocado in this recipe, try cocktail sauce. Here's a recipe for a homemade version.

Cocktail Sauce

1 cup ketchup

¼ cup prepared horseradish

1 lemon, zest and juice

dash Worcestershire sauce

dash or two Tabasco® sauce

1. Combine all ingredients in a bowl and enjoy!

Per Slider
Shrimp Slider with Avocado 350 Calories – 18g Fat (2.5g Sat. Fat) – 125mg Cholesterol – 31g Carbohydrates – 4g Fiber – 2g Sugar – 19g Protein
Cocktail Sauce 35 Calories – 0g Fat (0g Sat. Fat) – 0mg Cholesterol – 9g Carbohydrates – 0g Fiber – 8g Sugar – 1g Protein

Crab Stuffed Salmon Roast

Serves: **4 to 6** ■ Temperature: **370°F** ■ Cooking Time: **20 minutes**

1 (1½-pound) salmon fillet

salt and freshly ground black pepper

6 ounces crabmeat

1 teaspoon finely chopped lemon zest

1 teaspoon Dijon mustard

1 tablespoon chopped fresh parsley, plus more for garnish

1 scallion, chopped

¼ teaspoon salt

olive oil

GF

1. Prepare the salmon fillet by butterflying it. Slice into the thickest side of the salmon, parallel to the countertop and along the length of the fillet. Don't slice all the way through to the other side – stop about an inch from the edge. Open the salmon up like a book. Season the salmon with salt and freshly ground black pepper.

2. Make the crab filling by combining the crabmeat, lemon zest, mustard, parsley, scallion, salt and freshly ground black pepper in a bowl. Spread this filling in the center of the salmon. Fold one side of the salmon over the filling. Then fold the other side over on top.

3. Transfer the rolled salmon to the center of a piece of parchment paper that is roughly 6- to 7-inches wide and about 12-inches long. The parchment paper will act as a sling, making it easier to put the salmon into the air fryer. Pre-heat the air fryer to 370°F. Use the parchment paper to transfer the salmon roast to the air fryer basket and tuck the ends of the paper down beside the salmon. Drizzle a little olive oil on top and season with salt and pepper.

4. Air-fry the salmon at 370°F for 20 minutes.

5. Remove the roast from the air fryer and let it rest for a few minutes. Then, slice it, sprinkle some more lemon zest and parsley (or fresh chives) on top and serve.

Prep Help

Butterflying the salmon is the only tricky part of this recipe. Take your time as you try to get close to the other side of the salmon fillet, but stop before you cut through. When it's time to slice the finished roast, it's important to let the salmon rest for several minutes so that it sets up a little before you slice it with the sharpest knife you have.

Per Serving 440 Calories – 15g Fat (3g Sat. Fat) – 205mg Cholesterol – 1g Carbohydrates – 0g Fiber – 0g Sugar – 76g Protein

Step-by-Step Salmon Roast

1. Butterfly the salmon, but don't slice all the way through to the other side – stop about an inch from the edge.

2. Open the salmon up like a book.

3. Spread the crab filling in the center of the salmon.

4. Fold one side of the salmon over the filling.

5. Then fold the other side over on top.

6. Use parchment paper to transfer the salmon roast to the air fryer basket.

Crunchy and Buttery Cod with RITZ® Cracker Crust

Serves: 2 ■ Temperature: 380°F ■ Cooking Time: 8 to 10 minutes

Easy

4 tablespoons butter, melted

8 to 10 RITZ® crackers, crushed into crumbs

2 (6-ounce) cod fillets

salt and freshly ground black pepper

1 lemon

1. Pre-heat the air fryer to 380°F.

2. Melt the butter in a small saucepan on the stovetop or in a microwavable dish in the microwave, and then transfer the butter to a shallow dish. Place the crushed RITZ® crackers into a second shallow dish.

3. Season the fish fillets with salt and freshly ground black pepper. Dip them into the butter and then coat both sides with the RITZ® crackers.

4. Place the fish into the air fryer basket and air-fry at 380°F for 8 to 10 minutes, flipping the fish over halfway through the cooking time.

5. Serve with a wedge of lemon to squeeze over the top.

Note from Meredith

This is a classic New England preparation of fish. It's super easy and super tasty. The RITZ® crackers add even more buttery flavor to the cod, making it hard to resist and a family pleaser.

Per Serving 340 Calories – 21g Fat (12g Sat. Fat) – 120mg Cholesterol – 6g Carbohydrates – 0g Fiber – 1g Sugar – 31g Protein

Horseradish Crusted Salmon

Serves: **2** ■ Temperature: **360˚F** ■ Cooking Time: **12 to 14 minutes**

2 (5-ounce) salmon fillets

salt and freshly ground black pepper

2 teaspoons Dijon mustard

½ cup panko breadcrumbs*

2 tablespoons prepared horseradish

½ teaspoon finely chopped lemon zest

1 tablespoon olive oil

1 tablespoon chopped fresh parsley

*Make this recipe gluten free by using gluten-free panko breadcrumbs.

1. Pre-heat the air fryer to 360°F.

2. Season the salmon with salt and freshly ground black pepper. Then spread the Dijon mustard on the salmon, coating the entire surface.

3. Combine the breadcrumbs, horseradish, lemon zest and olive oil in a small bowl. Spread the mixture over the top of the salmon and press down lightly with your hands, adhering it to the salmon using the mustard as "glue".

4. Transfer the salmon to the air fryer basket and air-fry at 360°F for 12 to 14 minutes (depending on how thick your fillet is) or until the fish feels firm to the touch. Sprinkle with the parsley.

Easy

GF*

Note from Meredith
This is one of my favorite recipes for salmon. The horseradish and mustard add a little zing to the salmon, and the breadcrumb topping gives a nice crunch to every bite.

Per Serving 330 Calories – 16g Fat (2.5g Sat. Fat) – 80mg Cholesterol – 14g Carbohydrates – 1g Fiber – 2g Sugar – 30g Protein

Quick Shrimp Scampi

Serves: **2 to 4** ■ Temperature: **400°F** ■ Cooking Time: **5 minutes**

Easy

GF

16 to 20 raw large shrimp, peeled, deveined and tails removed

½ cup white wine

freshly ground black pepper

¼ cup + 1 tablespoon butter, divided

1 clove garlic, sliced

1 teaspoon olive oil

salt, to taste

juice of ½ lemon, to taste

¼ cup chopped fresh parsley

1. Start by marinating the shrimp in the white wine and freshly ground black pepper for at least 30 minutes, or as long as 2 hours in the refrigerator.

2. Pre-heat the air fryer to 400°F.

3. Melt ¼ cup of butter in a small saucepan on the stovetop. Add the garlic and let the butter simmer, but be sure to not let it burn.

4. Pour the shrimp and marinade into the air fryer, letting the marinade drain through to the bottom drawer. Drizzle the olive oil on the shrimp and season well with salt. Air-fry at 400°F for 3 minutes. Turn the shrimp over (don't shake the basket because the marinade will splash around) and pour the garlic butter over the shrimp. Air-fry for another 2 minutes.

5. Remove the shrimp from the air fryer basket and transfer them to a bowl. Squeeze lemon juice over all the shrimp and toss with the chopped parsley and remaining tablespoon of butter. Season to taste with salt and serve over rice or pasta, or on their own with some crusty bread.

Note from Meredith

Shrimp Scampi is probably the most widely known shrimp dish. It is often extremely garlicky and leaves its stamp with you for hours or days. I like to add only a little garlic by way of simmering sliced garlic with the butter before tossing the butter over the shrimp. That way, you can avoid eating the garlic if you don't like it. If you like more garlic, mince the garlic instead of slicing it and let the garlic coat the shrimp along with the butter.

Per Serving 120 Calories – 4.5g Fat (2g Sat. Fat) – 155mg Cholesterol – 2g Carbohydrates – 0g Fiber – 0g Sugar – 16g Protein

Lobster Tails with Lemon Garlic Butter

Serves: **2** ■ Temperature: **370°F** ■ Cooking Time: **5 minutes**

Easy

GF

4 ounces unsalted butter

1 tablespoon finely chopped lemon zest

1 clove garlic, thinly sliced

2 (6-ounce) lobster tails

salt and freshly ground black pepper

½ cup white wine

½ lemon, sliced

vegetable oil

1. Start by making the lemon garlic butter. Combine the butter, lemon zest and garlic in a small saucepan. Melt and simmer the butter on the stovetop over the lowest possible heat while you prepare the lobster tails.

2. Prepare the lobster tails by cutting down the middle of the top of the shell. Crack the bottom shell by squeezing the sides of the lobster together so that you can access the lobster meat inside. Pull the lobster tail up out of the shell, but leave it attached at the base of the tail. Lay the lobster meat on top of the shell and season with salt and freshly ground black pepper. Pour a little of the lemon garlic butter on top of the lobster meat and transfer the lobster to the refrigerator so that the butter solidifies a little.

3. Pour the white wine into the air fryer drawer and add the lemon slices. Pre-heat the air fryer to 400°F for 5 minutes.

4. Transfer the lobster tails to the air fryer basket. Air-fry at 370° for 5 minutes, brushing more butter on halfway through cooking. (Add a minute or two if your lobster tail is more than 6-ounces.) Remove and serve with more butter for dipping or drizzling.

Technique Tip

Cooking lobster doesn't get easier than this! The hardest part of this recipe is cutting the lobster shell and pulling the lobster meat out to rest on top, but if you are patient this will be easy once you get the hang of it. Once that prep step is done, the rest is a breeze. By adding liquid to the bottom of the air fryer and pre-heating for 5 minutes, you create a moist environment in which to cook the lobster, which helps to keep the lobster from drying out. If you don't want to use wine, try stock or even just water with the lemon slices.

Per Serving 580 Calories – 47g Fat (29g Sat. Fat) – 340mg Cholesterol – 4g Carbohydrates – 0g Fiber – 1g Sugar – 29g Protein

Vegetarian
Main Dishes

Spicy Vegetable and Tofu Shake Fry

Serves: **4 to 6** ■ Temperature: **400°F** ■ Cooking Time: **10 + 7 minutes**

GF*

Veg

4 teaspoons canola oil, divided

2 tablespoons rice wine vinegar

1 tablespoon sriracha chili sauce

¼ cup soy sauce*

½ teaspoon toasted sesame oil

1 teaspoon minced garlic

1 tablespoon minced fresh ginger

8 ounces extra firm tofu

½ cup vegetable stock or water

1 tablespoon honey

1 tablespoon cornstarch

½ red onion, chopped

1 red or yellow bell pepper, chopped

1 cup green beans, cut into 2-inch lengths

4 ounces mushrooms, sliced

2 scallions, sliced

2 tablespoons fresh cilantro leaves

2 teaspoons toasted sesame seeds

*Make this recipe gluten free by using a gluten-free soy sauce.

1. Combine 1 tablespoon of the oil, vinegar, sriracha sauce, soy sauce, sesame oil, garlic and ginger in a small bowl. Cut the tofu into bite-sized cubes and toss the tofu in with the marinade while you prepare the other vegetables. When you are ready to start cooking, remove the tofu from the marinade and set it aside. Add the water, honey and cornstarch to the marinade and bring to a simmer on the stovetop, just until the sauce thickens. Set the sauce aside.

2. Pre-heat the air fryer to 400°F.

3. Toss the onion, pepper, green beans and mushrooms in a bowl with a little canola oil and season with salt. Air-fry at 400°F for 10 to 12 minutes, shaking the basket and tossing the vegetables every few minutes. When the vegetables are cooked to your preferred doneness, remove them from the air fryer and set aside.

4. Add the tofu to the air fryer basket and air-fry at 400°F for 6 minutes, shaking the basket a few times during the cooking process. Add the vegetables back to the basket and air-fry for another minute. Transfer the vegetables and tofu to a large bowl, add the scallions and cilantro leaves and toss with the sauce. Serve over rice with sesame seeds sprinkled on top.

Note from Meredith

Yes, this is really a type of stir-fry, but since we shake the basket in air frying rather than stirring, I'm calling it a "shake fry"!

Per Serving 150 Calories – 8g Fat (6g Sat. Fat) – 0mg Cholesterol – 15g Carbohydrates – 2g Fiber – 6g Sugar – 8g Protein

Spaghetti Squash and Kale Fritters with Pomodoro Sauce

Serves: 3 ■ Temperature: 370°F ■ Cooking Time: 30 + 15 minutes

Veg
GF*

1½-pound spaghetti squash (about half a large or a whole small squash)

olive oil

½ onion, diced

½ red bell pepper, diced

2 cloves garlic, minced

4 cups coarsely chopped kale

salt and freshly ground black pepper

1 egg

⅓ cup breadcrumbs, divided*

⅓ cup grated Parmesan cheese

½ teaspoon dried rubbed sage

pinch nutmeg

*Make this recipe gluten free by using gluten-free breadcrumbs.

Pomodoro Sauce:

2 tablespoons olive oil

½ onion, chopped

1 to 2 cloves garlic, minced

1 (28-ounce) can peeled tomatoes

¼ cup red wine

1 teaspoon Italian seasoning

2 tablespoons chopped fresh basil, plus more for garnish

salt and freshly ground black pepper

½ teaspoon sugar (optional)

1. Pre-heat the air fryer to 370°F.

2. Cut the spaghetti squash in half lengthwise and remove the seeds. Rub the inside of the squash with olive oil and season with salt and pepper. Place the squash, cut side up, into the air fryer basket and air-fry for 30 minutes, flipping the squash over halfway through the cooking process.

3. While the squash is cooking, pre-heat a large sauté pan over medium heat on the stovetop. Add a little olive oil and sauté the onions for 3 minutes, until they start to soften. Add the red pepper and garlic and continue to sauté for an additional 4 minutes. Add the kale and season with salt and pepper. Cook for 2 more minutes, or until the kale is soft. Transfer the mixture to a large bowl and let it cool.

4. While the squash continues to cook, make the Pomodoro sauce. Pre-heat the large sauté pan again over medium heat on the stovetop. Add the olive oil and sauté the onion and garlic for 2 to 3 minutes, until the onion begins to soften. Crush the canned tomatoes with your hands and add them to the pan along with the red wine and Italian seasoning and simmer for 20 minutes. Add the basil and season to taste with salt, pepper and sugar (if using).

5. When the spaghetti squash has finished cooking, use a fork to scrape the inside flesh of the squash onto a sheet pan. Spread the squash out and let it cool.

6. Once cool, add the spaghetti squash to the kale mixture, along with the egg, breadcrumbs, Parmesan cheese, sage, nutmeg, salt and freshly ground black pepper. Stir to combine well and then divide the mixture into 6 thick portions. You can shape the portions into patties, but I prefer to keep them a little random and unique in shape. Spray or brush the fritters with olive oil.

7. Pre-heat the air fryer to 370°F.

8. Brush the air fryer basket with a little olive oil and transfer the fritters to the basket. Air-fry the squash and kale fritters at 370°F for 15 minutes, flipping them over halfway through the cooking process.

9. Serve the fritters warm with the Pomodoro sauce spooned over the top or pooled on your plate. Garnish with the fresh basil leaves.

Per Serving 260 Calories – 9g Fat (3g Sat. Fat) – 10mg Cholesterol – 38g Carbohydrates – 6g Fiber – 9g Sugar – 10g Protein

Short Cut

If you want to speed this recipe up a little and save time, you can cook the spaghetti squash in the microwave. Simply brush the cut side of the spaghetti squash with a little olive oil and season with salt and pepper. Place the spaghetti squash halves, cut side down, in a microwave-safe casserole dish. Microwave for 8 to 12 minutes, depending on the strength of your microwave and the size of the squash.

Mushroom and Fried Onion Quesadilla

Serves: **2 to 4** ■ Temperature: **400°F** ■ Cooking Time: **25 + 8 minutes**

Easy

Veg

1 onion, sliced

2 tablespoons butter, melted

10 ounces button mushrooms, sliced

2 tablespoons Worcestershire sauce

salt and freshly ground black pepper

4 (8-inch) flour tortillas

2 cups grated Fontina cheese

vegetable or olive oil

1. Pre-heat the air fryer to 400°F.

2. Toss the onion slices with the melted butter and transfer them to the air fryer basket. Air-fry at 400°F for 15 minutes, shaking the basket several times during the cooking process. Add the mushrooms and Worcestershire sauce to the onions and stir to combine. Air-fry at 400°F for an additional 10 minutes. Season with salt and freshly ground black pepper.

3. Lay two of the tortillas on a cutting board. Top each tortilla with ½ cup of the grated cheese, half of the onion and mushroom mixture and then finally another ½ cup of the cheese. Place the remaining tortillas on top of the cheese and press down firmly.

4. Brush the air fryer basket with a little oil. Place a quesadilla in the basket and brush the top with a little oil. Secure the top tortilla to the bottom with three toothpicks and air-fry at 400°F for 5 minutes. Flip the quesadilla over by inverting it onto a plate and sliding it back into the basket. Remove the toothpicks and brush the other side with oil. Air-fry for an additional 3 minutes.

5. Invert the quesadilla onto a cutting board and cut it into 4 or 6 triangles. Serve with sour cream and salsa (or try the chutney below).

Cranberry Chutney

olive oil

½ onion, diced

2 Jalapeño peppers, diced

1 (14-ounce) can whole-berry cranberry sauce

1 teaspoon chili powder

¼ cup water

1. Pre-heat a sauté pan over medium-high heat on the stove-top. Add the oil and sauté the onion slices for 5 minutes, until they brown. Add the Jalapeño peppers and cook for another minute. Add the cranberry sauce, chili powder and water and simmer for 15 minutes. Season with salt and fresh ground black pepper. Let the chutney sit at room temperature until you are ready to serve.

Serving Suggestion

You can serve the quesadilla with standard salsa, but this easy cranberry chutney is a surprisingly nice alternative.

Per Serving
Mushroom Quesadilla 350 Calories – 24g Fat 14g Sat. Fat) – 80mg Cholesterol – 17g Carbohydrates – 2g Fiber – 3g Sugar – 18g Protein
Cranberry Chutney 160 Calories – 0g Fat (0g Sat. Fat) – 0mg Cholesterol – 40g Carbohydrates – 1g Fiber – 32g Sugar – 0g Protein

Corn and Pepper Jack Chile Rellenos with Roasted Tomato Sauce

Serves: 3 to 4 ■ Temperature: 400°F + 350°F ■ Cooking Time: 10 + 10 + 10 minutes

Veg

GF*

3 Poblano peppers

1 cup all-purpose flour*

salt and freshly ground black pepper

2 eggs, lightly beaten

1 cup plain breadcrumbs*

olive oil, in a spray bottle

Sauce

2 cups cherry tomatoes

1 Jalapeño pepper, halved and seeded

1 clove garlic

¼ red onion, broken into large pieces

1 tablespoon olive oil

salt, to taste

2 tablespoons chopped fresh cilantro

Filling

olive oil

¼ red onion, finely chopped

1 teaspoon minced garlic

1 cup corn kernels, fresh or frozen

2 cups grated pepper jack cheese

*Make this recipe gluten free by using gluten-free flour and gluten-free breadcrumbs.

1. Start by roasting the peppers. Pre-heat the air fryer to 400°F. Place the peppers into the air fryer basket and air-fry at 400°F for 10 minutes, turning them over halfway through the cooking time. Remove the peppers from the basket and cover loosely with foil.

2. While the peppers are cooling, make the roasted tomato sauce. Place all sauce ingredients except for the cilantro into the air fryer basket and air-fry at 400°F for 10 minutes, shaking the basket once or twice. When the sauce ingredients have finished air-frying, transfer everything to a blender or food processor and blend or process to a smooth sauce, adding a little warm water to get the desired consistency. Season to taste with salt, add the cilantro and set aside.

3. While the sauce ingredients are cooking in the air fryer, make the filling. Heat a skillet on the stovetop over medium heat. Add the olive oil and sauté the red onion and garlic for 4 to 5 minutes. Transfer the onion and garlic to a bowl, stir in the corn and cheese, and set aside.

4. Set up a dredging station with three shallow dishes. Place the flour, seasoned with salt and pepper, in the first shallow dish. Place the eggs in the second dish, and fill the third shallow dish with the breadcrumbs. When the peppers have cooled, carefully slice into one side of the pepper to create an opening. Pull the seeds out of the peppers and peel away the skins, trying not to tear the pepper. Fill each pepper with some of the corn and cheese filling and close the pepper up again by folding one side of the opening over the other. Carefully roll each pepper in the seasoned flour, then into the egg and finally into the breadcrumbs to coat on all sides, trying not to let the pepper fall open. Spray the peppers on all sides with a little olive oil.

5. Air-fry two peppers at a time at 350°F for 6 minutes. Turn the peppers over and air-fry for another 4 minutes. Serve the peppers warm on a bed of the roasted tomato sauce.

Per Serving 390 Calories – 22g Fat (11g Sat. Fat) – 80mg Cholesterol – 34g Carbohydrates – 5g Fiber – 5g Sugar – 20g Protein

Note from Meredith
These peppers can be a little tricky to stuff and coat without tearing them. Do yourself a favor and choose large unblemished peppers at the grocery store. Then, forgive yourself if you do tear the pepper – you can always piece it back together again and often you can use the breading to patch any holes or cracks.

Cucumber Dill Yogurt Sauce

1 cup grated cucumber (about 1 medium
cucumber, seeds removed)

1 cup Greek yogurt

2 teaspoons lemon juice

¼ teaspoon salt

freshly ground black pepper

1 tablespoon chopped fresh dills

1 tablespoon olive oil

1. Mix all ingredients together in a bowl.

Quinoa Burgers with Feta Cheese and Dill

Serves: **6** ■ Temperature: **400˚F** ■ Cooking Time: **10 minutes per batch**

1 cup quinoa (red, white or multi-colored)

1½ cups water

1 teaspoon salt

freshly ground black pepper

1½ cups rolled oats

3 eggs, lightly beaten

¼ cup minced white onion

½ cup crumbled feta cheese

¼ cup chopped fresh dill

salt and freshly ground black pepper

vegetable or canola oil, in a spray bottle

whole-wheat hamburger buns
(or gluten-free hamburger buns*)

arugula

tomato, sliced

red onion, sliced

mayonnaise

*These burger patties are gluten free. If you choose a gluten-free hamburger bun, then your whole meal can be gluten free too.

1. Make the quinoa: Rinse the quinoa in cold water in a saucepan, swirling it with your hand until any dry husks rise to the surface. Drain the quinoa as well as you can and then put the saucepan on the stovetop to dry and toast the quinoa. Turn the heat to medium-high and shake the pan regularly until you see the quinoa moving easily and can hear the seeds moving in the pan, indicating that they are dry. Add the water, salt and pepper. Bring the liquid to a boil and then reduce the heat to low or medium-low. You should see just a few bubbles, not a boil. Cover with a lid, leaving it askew and simmer for 20 minutes. Turn the heat off and fluff the quinoa with a fork. If there's any liquid left in the bottom of the pot, place it back on the burner for another 3 minutes or so. Spread the cooked quinoa out on a sheet pan to cool.

2. Combine the room temperature quinoa in a large bowl with the oats, eggs, onion, cheese and dill. Season with salt and pepper and mix well (remember that feta cheese is salty). Shape the mixture into 6 patties with flat sides (so they fit more easily into the air fryer). Add a little water or a few more rolled oats if necessary to get the mixture to be the right consistency to make patties.

3. Pre-heat the air-fryer to 400°F.

4. Spray both sides of the patties generously with oil and transfer them to the air fryer basket in one layer (you will probably have to cook these burgers in batches, depending on the size of your air fryer). Air-fry each batch at 400°F for 10 minutes, flipping the burgers over halfway through the cooking time.

5. Build your burger on the whole-wheat hamburger buns with arugula, tomato, red onion and mayonnaise (or the cucumber dill yogurt sauce on the opposite page).

GF*

Veg

Per Serving
Quinoa Burger 560 Calories - 14g Fat (3.5g Sat. Fat) - 105mg Cholesterol - 88g Carbohydrates - 7g Fiber - 9g Sugar - 22g Protein
Cucumber Dill Yogurt Sauce 80 Calories - 6g Fat (2.5g Sat. Fat) - 15mg Cholesterol - 4g Carbohydrates - 0g Fiber - 2g Sugar - 3g Protein

Roasted Vegetable Thai Green Curry

Serves: **4** ■ Temperature: **400˚F** ■ Cooking Time: **16 minutes**

1 (13-ounce) can coconut milk

3 tablespoons green curry paste

1 tablespoon soy sauce*

1 tablespoon rice wine vinegar

1 teaspoon sugar

1 teaspoon minced fresh ginger

½ onion, chopped

3 carrots, sliced

1 red bell pepper, chopped

olive oil

10 stalks of asparagus, cut into 2-inch pieces

3 cups broccoli florets

basmati rice for serving

fresh cilantro

crushed red pepper flakes (optional)

*Make this recipe gluten free by using a gluten-free soy sauce.

Easy

GF*

Veg

1. Combine the coconut milk, green curry paste, soy sauce, rice wine vinegar, sugar and ginger in a medium saucepan and bring to a boil on the stovetop. Reduce the heat and simmer for 20 minutes while you cook the vegetables. Set aside.

2. Pre-heat the air fryer to 400°F.

3. Toss the onion, carrots, and red pepper together with a little olive oil and transfer the vegetables to the air fryer basket. Air-fry at 400°F for 10 minutes, shaking the basket a few times during the cooking process. Add the asparagus and broccoli florets and air-fry for an additional 6 minutes, again shaking the basket for even cooking.

4. When the vegetables are cooked to your liking, toss them with the green curry sauce and serve in bowls over basmati rice. Garnish with fresh chopped cilantro and crushed red pepper flakes.

Dress It Up
You can add some protein to this dish by air-frying some tofu to toss in. Marinate the tofu in some of the curry sauce for 10 minutes or so. Then air fry at 400°F for 6 minutes until lightly browned on the edges. It's a delicious add!

Per Serving 270 Calories – 20g Fat (12g Sat. Fat) – 0mg Cholesterol – 16g Carbohydrates – 4g Fiber – 8g Sugar – 5g Protein

Parmesan Portobello Mushroom Caps

Serves: **2** ■ Temperature: **400˚F + 350˚F** ■ Cooking Time: **14 minutes**

Easy

Veg

GF*

¼ cup flour*

1 egg, lightly beaten

1 cup seasoned breadcrumbs*

2 large portobello mushroom caps, stems and gills removed

olive oil, in a spray bottle

½ cup tomato sauce

¾ cup grated mozzarella cheese

1 tablespoon grated Parmesan cheese

1 tablespoon chopped fresh basil or parsley

*Make this recipe gluten free by using gluten-free flour and gluten-free breadcrumbs.

1. Set up a dredging station with three shallow dishes. Place the flour in the first shallow dish, egg in the second dish and breadcrumbs in the last dish. Dredge the mushrooms in flour, then dip them into the egg and finally press them into the breadcrumbs to coat on all sides. Spray both sides of the coated mushrooms with olive oil.

2. Pre-heat the air fryer to 400°F.

3. Air-fry the mushrooms at 400°F for 10 minutes, turning them over halfway through the cooking process.

4. Fill the underside of the mushrooms with the tomato sauce and then top the sauce with the mozzarella and Parmesan cheeses. Reset the air fryer temperature to 350°F and air-fry for an additional 4 minutes, until the cheese has melted and is slightly browned.

5. Serve the mushrooms with pasta tossed with tomato sauce and garnish with some chopped fresh basil or parsley.

Prep Help
Use a large spoon to remove the gills from the underside of the mushroom. Simply scoop the dark gills out and discard. While the gills are completely edible, they tend to turn everything a dark color, plus removing them will give you more room for sauce and cheese.

Per Serving 290 Calories – 12g Fat (6g Sat. Fat) – 65mg Cholesterol – 29g Carbohydrates – 3g Fiber – 7g Sugar – 16g Protein

General Tso's Cauliflower

Serves: **4** ■ Temperature: **400°F** ■ Cooking Time: **15 minutes**

Easy

Veg

GF*

1 head cauliflower cut into florets

¾ cup all-purpose flour, divided*

3 eggs, lightly beaten

1 cup panko breadcrumbs*

canola or peanut oil, in a spray bottle

2 tablespoons oyster sauce

¼ cup soy sauce

2 teaspoons chili paste

2 tablespoons rice wine vinegar

2 tablespoons sugar

¼ cup water

white or brown rice for serving

steamed broccoli

*Make this recipe gluten free by using gluten-free flour and gluten-free breadcrumbs.

1. Set up dredging station using three bowls. Place the cauliflower in a large bowl and sprinkle ¼ cup of the flour over the top. Place the eggs in a second bowl and combine the panko breadcrumbs and remaining ½ cup flour in a third bowl. Toss the cauliflower in the flour to coat all the florets thoroughly. Dip the cauliflower florets in the eggs and finally toss them in the breadcrumbs to coat on all sides. Place the coated cauliflower florets on a baking sheet and spray generously with canola or peanut oil.

2. Pre-heat the air fryer to 400°F.

3. Air-fry the cauliflower at 400°F for 15 minutes, flipping the florets over for the last 3 minutes of the cooking process and spraying again with oil.

4. While the cauliflower is air-frying, make the General Tso Sauce. Combine the oyster sauce, soy sauce, chili paste, rice wine vinegar, sugar and water in a saucepan and bring the mixture to a boil on the stovetop. Lower the heat and let it simmer for 10 minutes, stirring occasionally.

5. When the timer is up on the air fryer, transfer the cauliflower to a large bowl, pour the sauce over it all and toss to coat. Serve with white or brown rice and some steamed broccoli.

Note from Meredith

Here's a great way to get your Chinese food fix right at home and keep it vegetarian. Cut the cauliflower florets into bite-sized pieces – especially if you intend to eat this with chopsticks!

Per Serving 90 Calories – 1.5g Fat (0g Sat. Fat) – 30mg Cholesterol – 15g Carbohydrates – 2g Fiber – 5g Sugar – 4g Protein

Rigatoni with Roasted Onions, Fennel, Spinach and Lemon Pepper Ricotta

Serves: **2 to 3** ■ Temperature: **400°F** ■ Cooking Time: **13 minutes**

Easy

Veg

1 red onion, rough chopped into large chunks

2 teaspoons olive oil, divided

1 bulb fennel, sliced ¼-inch thick

¾ cup ricotta cheese

1½ teaspoons finely chopped lemon zest, plus more for garnish

1 teaspoon lemon juice

salt and freshly ground black pepper

8 ounces (½ pound) dried rigatoni pasta

3 cups baby spinach leaves

1. Bring a large stockpot of salted water to a boil on the stovetop and pre-heat the air fryer to 400°F.

2. While the water is coming to a boil, toss the chopped onion in 1 teaspoon of olive oil and transfer to the air fryer basket. Air-fry at 400°F for 5 minutes. Toss the sliced fennel with 1 teaspoon of olive oil and add this to the air fryer basket with the onions. Continue to air-fry at 400°F for 8 minutes, shaking the basket a few times during the cooking process.

3. Combine the ricotta cheese, lemon zest and juice, ¼ teaspoon of salt and freshly ground black pepper in a bowl and stir until smooth.

4. Add the dried rigatoni to the boiling water and cook according to the package directions. When the pasta is cooked al dente, reserve one cup of the pasta water and drain the pasta into a colander.

5. Place the spinach in a serving bowl and immediately transfer the hot pasta to the bowl, wilting the spinach. Add the roasted onions and fennel and toss together. Add a little pasta water to the dish if it needs moistening. Then, dollop the lemon pepper ricotta cheese on top and nestle it into the hot pasta. Garnish with more lemon zest if desired.

Make It Your Own

This recipe is a nice template for numerous pasta dishes. It's so easy to air-fry some vegetables and toss with some pasta and cheese for a quick weekday dinner. Remember to reserve some of the pasta water to moisten the finished dish if necessary.

Per Serving 400 Calories – 11 Fat (3.5g Sat. Fat) – 20mg Cholesterol – 62g Carbohydrates – 6g Fiber – 8g Sugar – 16g Protein

Roasted Vegetable, Brown Rice and Black Bean Burrito

Serves: 2 ■ Temperature: 400°F + 360°F ■ Cooking Time: 12 + 8 minutes

Veg

½ zucchini, sliced ¼-inch thick

½ red onion, sliced

1 yellow bell pepper, sliced

2 teaspoons olive oil

salt and freshly ground black pepper

2 burrito size flour tortillas

1 cup grated pepper jack cheese

½ cup cooked brown rice

½ cup canned black beans, drained and rinsed

¼ teaspoon ground cumin

1 tablespoon chopped fresh cilantro

fresh salsa, guacamole and sour cream, for serving

1. Pre-heat the air fryer to 400°F.

2. Toss the vegetables in a bowl with the olive oil, salt and freshly ground black pepper. Air-fry at 400°F for 12 to 15 minutes, shaking the basket a few times during the cooking process. The vegetables are done when they are cooked to your liking.

3. In the meantime, start building the burritos. Lay the tortillas out on the counter. Sprinkle half of the cheese in the center of the tortillas. Combine the rice, beans, cumin and cilantro in a bowl, season to taste with salt and freshly ground black pepper and then divide the mixture between the two tortillas. When the vegetables have finished cooking, transfer them to the two tortillas, placing the vegetables on top of the rice and beans. Sprinkle the remaining cheese on top and then roll the burritos up, tucking in the sides of the tortillas as you roll. Brush or spray the outside of the burritos with olive oil and transfer them to the air fryer.

4. Air-fry at 360°F for 8 minutes, turning them over when there are about 2 minutes left. The burritos will have slightly brown spots, but will still be pliable.

5. Serve with some fresh salsa, guacamole and sour cream.

Serving Suggestion
A nice addition to this meal would be some air-fried tortilla chips to snatch up the extra salsa and guacamole!

Corn Tortilla Chips

10- or 8-inch corn tortillas, cut into wedges

vegetable oil

salt

1. Pre-heat the air fryer to 380°F.

2. Spray or brush the tortilla triangles with the oil and transfer them to the air fryer basket. Don't overfill the air fryer basket, but fry in batches. Air-fry for 5 minutes, shaking the basket once or twice during the cooking time to redistribute the chips.

3. Season the chips with salt as soon as they are finished.

Per Roasted Vegetable Burrito 520 Calories - 26g Fat (12g Sat. Fat) - 50mg Cholesterol - 52g Carbohydrates - 8g Fiber - 5g Sugar - 22g Protein

Mexican Twice Air-Fried Sweet Potatoes

Serves: 2 ■ Temperature: 400˚F + 370˚F + 340˚F ■ Cooking Time: 30 + 12 minutes

GF

Veg

2 large sweet potatoes

olive oil

salt and freshly ground black pepper

⅓ cup diced red onion

⅓ cup diced red bell pepper

½ cup canned black beans, drained and rinsed

½ cup corn kernels, fresh or frozen

½ teaspoon chili powder

1½ cups grated pepper jack cheese, divided

Jalapeño peppers, sliced

1. Pre-heat the air fryer to 400°F.

2. Rub the outside of the sweet potatoes with olive oil and season with salt and freshly ground black pepper. Transfer the potatoes into the air fryer basket and air-fry at 400°F for 30 minutes, rotating the potatoes a few times during the cooking process.

3. While the potatoes are air-frying, start the potato filling. Pre-heat a large sauté pan over medium heat on the stovetop. Add the onion and pepper and sauté for a few minutes, until the vegetables start to soften. Add the black beans, corn, and chili powder and sauté for another 3 minutes. Set the mixture aside.

4. Remove the sweet potatoes from the air fryer and let them rest for 5 minutes. Slice off one inch of the flattest side of both potatoes. Scrape the potato flesh out of the potatoes, leaving half an inch of potato flesh around the edge of the potato. Place all the potato flesh into a large bowl and mash it with a fork. Add the black bean mixture and 1 cup of the pepper jack cheese to the mashed sweet potatoes. Season with salt and freshly ground black pepper and mix well. Stuff the hollowed out potato shells with the black bean and sweet potato mixture, mounding the filling high in the potatoes.

5. Transfer the stuffed potatoes back into the air fryer basket and air-fry at 370°F for 10 minutes. Sprinkle the remaining cheese on top of each stuffed potato, lower the heat to 340°F and air-fry for an additional 2 minutes to melt the cheese. Top with a couple slices of Jalapeño pepper and serve warm with a green salad.

Serving Suggestion
You could make this recipe with smaller sweet potatoes as a tasty side dish too!

Per Serving 960 Calories – 53g Fat (26g Sat. Fat) – 125mg Cholesterol – 91g Carbohydrates – 19g Fiber – 16g Sugar – 44g Protein

Vegetables

Jerk Rubbed Corn on the Cob

Serves: **4** ■ Temperature: **380°F** ■ Cooking Time: **6 minutes**

1 teaspoon ground allspice

1 teaspoon dried thyme

½ teaspoon ground ginger

½ teaspoon ground cinnamon

¼ teaspoon ground nutmeg

⅛ teaspoon ground cayenne pepper

1 teaspoon salt

2 tablespoons butter, melted

4 ears of corn, husked

1. Pre-heat the air fryer to 380°F.

2. Combine all the spices in a bowl. Brush the corn with the melted butter and then sprinkle the spices generously on all sides of each ear of corn.

3. Transfer the ears of corn to the air fryer basket. It's ok if they are crisscrossed on top of each other. Air-fry at 380°F for 6 minutes, rotating the ears as they cook.

4. Brush more butter on at the end and sprinkle with any remaining spice mixture.

Easy

Veg

GF

Substitution Tip

A wet jerk rub will be much spicier than the version above. If you're a pepper-hound and love foods as spicy as possible, blend the following ingredients together in a mini food processor and brush the mixture on the corn before air-frying. Air-fry at 380°F for 6 minutes as above. (This wet rub is also great on chicken!)

> 1 teaspoon brown sugar
> 1 teaspoon ground allspice
> 1 teaspoon dried thyme
> ½ teaspoon ground ginger
> ½ teaspoon ground cinnamon
> ¼ teaspoon ground nutmeg
> 3 cloves garlic
> 4 green onions, roughly chopped
> 1 Habeñero pepper, stem and seeds removed (unless you're a devil!)
> juice of 1 lime
> 1 teaspoon salt

Per Serving 110 Calories – 6g Fat (3.5g Sat. Fat) – 15mg Cholesterol – 15g Carbohydrates – 2g Fiber – 2g Sugar – 2g Protein

Latkes

Makes: **12 Latkes** ■ Temperature: **400°F** ■ Cooking Time: **13 minutes per batch**

Veg

GF*

1 russet potato

¼ onion

2 eggs, lightly beaten

⅓ cup flour*

½ teaspoon baking powder

1 teaspoon salt

freshly ground black pepper

canola or vegetable oil,
in a spray bottle

chopped chives, for garnish

apple sauce

sour cream

*Make this recipe gluten free by using
gluten-free flour.

1. Shred the potato and onion with a coarse box grater or a food processor with the shredding blade. Place the shredded vegetables into a colander or mesh strainer and squeeze or press down firmly to remove the excess water.

2. Transfer the onion and potato to a large bowl and add the eggs, flour, baking powder, salt and black pepper. Mix to combine and then shape the mixture into patties, about ¼-cup of mixture each. Brush or spray both sides of the latkes with oil.

3. Pre-heat the air fryer to 400°F.

4. Air-fry the latkes in batches. Transfer one layer of the latkes to the air fryer basket and air-fry at 400°F for 12 to 13 minutes, flipping them over halfway through the cooking time. Transfer the finished latkes to a platter and cover with aluminum foil, or place them in a warm oven to keep warm.

5. Garnish the latkes with chopped chives and serve with sour cream and applesauce.

Make it Ahead

You can make these latkes ahead of time and then easily re-heat them by returning them to the air fryer at 370°F for 5 minutes, rotating them halfway through the re-heating process.

Per Latke 60 Calories – 1g Fat (0g Sat. Fat) – 15mg Cholesterol – 12g Carbohydrates – 1g Fiber – 0g Sugar – 2g Protein

Summer Vegetables with Balsamic Drizzle, Goat Cheese and Basil

Serves: **2** ▪ Temperature: **390˚F** ▪ Cooking Time: **17 minutes**

1 cup balsamic vinegar

1 zucchini, sliced

1 yellow squash, sliced

2 tablespoons olive oil

1 clove garlic, minced

½ teaspoon Italian seasoning

salt and freshly ground black pepper

½ cup cherry tomatoes, halved

2 ounces crumbled goat cheese

2 tablespoons chopped fresh basil, plus more leaves for garnish

1. Place the balsamic vinegar in a small saucepot on the stovetop. Bring the vinegar to a boil, lower the heat and simmer uncovered for 20 minutes, until the mixture reduces and thickens. Set aside to cool.

2. Pre-heat the air fryer to 390°F.

3. Combine the zucchini and yellow squash in a large bowl. Add the olive oil, minced garlic, Italian seasoning, salt and pepper and toss to coat.

4. Air-fry the vegetables at 390°F for 10 minutes, shaking the basket several times during the cooking process. Add the cherry tomatoes and continue to air-fry for another 5 minutes. Sprinkle the goat cheese over the vegetables and air-fry for 2 more minutes.

5. Transfer the vegetables to a serving dish, drizzle with the balsamic reduction and season with freshly ground black pepper. Garnish with the fresh basil leaves.

Make it Easy

To make this a super quick recipe, skip step #1 and buy a bottle of balsamic glaze from your grocery store. Do not pass 'GO', do not collect $200, go straight to step #2!

Per Serving 360 Calories – 19g Fat (6g Sat. Fat) – 25mg Cholesterol – 37g Carbohydrates – 3g Fiber – 23g Sugar – 8g Protein

Fried Green Tomatoes with Sriracha Mayo

Serves: **4** ■ Temperature: **400˚F / 350˚F** ■ Cooking Time: **12 minutes per batch**

Easy

Veg

GF*

3 green tomatoes

salt and freshly ground black pepper

⅓ cup all-purpose flour*

2 eggs

½ cup buttermilk

1 cup panko breadcrumbs*

1 cup cornmeal

olive oil, in a spray bottle

fresh thyme sprigs or
chopped fresh chives

*Make this recipe gluten free by using gluten-free flour and gluten-free panko breadcrumbs.

Sriracha Mayo

½ cup mayonnaise

1 to 2 tablespoons sriracha hot sauce

1 tablespoon milk

1. Cut the tomatoes in ¼-inch slices. Pat them dry with a clean kitchen towel and season generously with salt and pepper.

2. Set up a dredging station using three shallow dishes. Place the flour in the first shallow dish, whisk the eggs and buttermilk together in the second dish, and combine the panko breadcrumbs and cornmeal in the third dish.

3. Pre-heat the air fryer to 400°F.

4. Dredge the tomato slices in flour to coat on all sides. Then dip them into the egg mixture and finally press them into the breadcrumbs to coat all sides of the tomato.

5. Spray or brush the air-fryer basket with olive oil. Transfer 3 to 4 tomato slices into the basket and spray the top with olive oil. Air-fry the tomatoes at 400°F for 8 minutes. Flip them over, spray the other side with oil and air-fry for an additional 4 minutes until golden brown.

6. While the tomatoes are cooking, make the sriracha mayo. Combine the mayonnaise, 1 tablespoon of the sriracha hot sauce and milk in a small bowl. Stir well until the mixture is smooth. Add more sriracha sauce to taste.

7. When the tomatoes are done, transfer them to a cooling rack or a platter lined with paper towels so the bottom does not get soggy. Before serving, carefully stack the all the tomatoes into air fryer and air-fry at 350°F for 1 to 2 minutes to heat them back up.

8. Serve the fried green tomatoes hot with the sriracha mayo on the side. Season one last time with salt and freshly ground black pepper and garnish with sprigs of fresh thyme or chopped fresh chives.

Dress It Up

Make this recipe in the summer when tomatoes are in season and most stores carry green tomatoes, or better yet pick them early from your own garden. A simple and nice way to dress these up is to top each finished fried tomato slice with some fresh crabmeat and drizzle the sriracha mayonnaise on top. Garnish it with some chopped dill and a lemon wedge, and you might even impress yourself!

Per Serving
Fried Green Tomatoes 340 Calories – 5g Fat (2g Sat. Fat) – 55mg Cholesterol – 62g Carbohydrates – 5g Fiber – 9g Sugar – 12g Protein
Sriracha Mayo 190 Calories – 21g Fat (3.5g Sat. Fat) – 10mg Cholesterol – 1g Carbohydrates – 0g Fiber – 1g Sugar – 0g Protein

Curried Cauliflower with Cashews and Yogurt

Serves: **2** ■ Temperature: **400°F** ■ Cooking Time: **12 minutes**

4 cups cauliflower florets
(about half a large head)

1 tablespoon olive oil

salt

1 teaspoon curry powder

½ cup toasted, chopped cashews

Cool Yogurt Drizzle

¼ cup plain yogurt

2 tablespoons sour cream

1 teaspoon lemon juice

pinch cayenne pepper

salt

1 teaspoon honey

1 tablespoon chopped fresh cilantro,
plus leaves for garnish

1. Pre-heat the air fryer to 400°F.

2. Toss the cauliflower florets with the olive oil, salt and curry powder, coating evenly.

3. Transfer the cauliflower to the air fryer basket and air-fry at 400°F for 12 minutes, shaking the basket a couple of times during the cooking process.

4. While the cauliflower is cooking, make the cool yogurt drizzle by combining all ingredients in a bowl.

5. When the cauliflower is cooked to your liking, serve it warm with the cool yogurt either underneath or drizzled over the top. Scatter the cashews and cilantro leaves around.

Turn into an Appetizer

You can turn this side dish into an appetizing dip by combining the yogurt drizzle and the cauliflower in a food processor or blender. Purée everything together, adding a little olive oil to get it to the right consistency. Serve with naan or pita chips, or some crudité vegetables.

Per Serving
Curried Cauliflower 270 Calories – 21g Fat (3.5g Sat. Fat) – 50mg Cholesterol – 18g Carbohydrates – 5g Fiber – 5g Sugar – 9g Protein
Cool Yogurt Drizzle 60 Calories – 3.5g Fat (2g Sat. Fat) – 30mg Cholesterol – 6g Carbohydrates – 0g Fiber – 5g Sugar – 2g Protein

Butternut Medallions with Honey Butter and Sage

Serves: **2 to 3** ◼ Temperature: **370˚F** ◼ Cooking Time: **15 minutes per batch**

Easy
GF
Veg

1 butternut squash, peeled

olive oil, in a spray bottle

salt and freshly ground black pepper

2 tablespoons butter, softened

2 tablespoons honey

pinch ground cinnamon

pinch ground nutmeg

chopped fresh sage

1. Pre-heat the air fryer to 370°F.

2. Cut the neck of the butternut squash into disks about ½-inch thick. (Use the base of the butternut squash for another use.) Brush or spray the disks with oil and season with salt and freshly ground black pepper.

3. Transfer the butternut disks to the air fryer in one layer (or just ever so slightly overlapping). Air-fry at 370°F for 5 minutes.

4. While the butternut squash is cooking, combine the butter, honey, cinnamon and nutmeg in a small bowl. Brush this mixture on the butternut squash, flip the disks over and brush the other side as well. Continue to air-fry at 370°F for another 5 minutes. Flip the disks once more, brush with more of the honey butter and air-fry for another 5 minutes. The butternut should be browning nicely around the edges.

5. Remove the butternut squash from the air-fryer and repeat with additional batches if necessary. Transfer to a serving platter, sprinkle with the fresh sage and serve.

Note from Meredith

This recipe calls for only the neck of the butternut squash because you can get nice slices from the neck. That doesn't mean that you can't make the same honey-butter butternut squash with the flesh of butternut that surrounds the seeds at the bottom of the vegetable – it just won't be as pretty. You can also cut the bottom of the butternut squash into chunks and air-fry them with salt and pepper for salads, pasta or just another (not-so-pretty) side dish.

Per Serving 310 Calories – 8g Fat (4.5g Sat. Fat) – 20mg Cholesterol – 63g Carbohydrates – 9g Fiber – 20g Sugar – 5g Protein

Smashed Fried Baby Potatoes

Serves: **3 to 4** ■ Temperature: **400°F** ■ Cooking Time: **18 minutes per batch**

GF

Veg

1½ pounds baby red or
baby Yukon gold potatoes

¼ cup butter, melted

1 teaspoon olive oil

½ teaspoon paprika

1 teaspoon dried parsley

salt and freshly ground black pepper

2 scallions, finely chopped

1. Bring a large pot of salted water to a boil. Add the potatoes and boil for 18 minutes or until the potatoes are fork-tender.

2. Drain the potatoes and transfer them to a cutting board to cool slightly. Spray or brush the bottom of a drinking glass with a little oil. Smash or flatten the potatoes by pressing the glass down on each potato slowly. Try not to completely flatten the potato or smash it so hard that it breaks apart.

3. Combine the melted butter, olive oil, paprika, and parsley together.

4. Pre-heat the air fryer to 400°F.

5. Spray the bottom of the air fryer basket with oil and transfer one layer of the smashed potatoes into the basket. Brush with some of the butter mixture and season generously with salt and freshly ground black pepper.

6. Air-fry at 400°F for 10 minutes. Carefully flip the potatoes over and air-fry for an additional 8 minutes until crispy and lightly browned.

7. Keep the potatoes warm in a 170°F oven or tent with aluminum foil while you cook the second batch. Sprinkle minced scallions over the potatoes and serve warm.

Technique Tip

These fried potatoes do need to be air-fried in batches in order to get the crispiest result. You can always pop the first batch back in with the second batch for the last couple of minutes to re-heat them, hold them warm in an oven OR just enjoy them right out of the fryer and come back for seconds when the next batch is done.

Per Serving 240 Calories – 14g Fat (7g Sat. Fat) – 30mg Cholesterol –
28g Carbohydrates – 4g Fiber – 2g Sugar – 4g Protein

Roasted Heirloom Carrots with Orange and Thyme

Serves: 2 ■ Temperature: 400°F ■ Cooking Time: 12 minutes

10 to 12 heirloom or rainbow carrots (about 1 pound), scrubbed but not peeled

1 teaspoon olive oil

salt and freshly ground black pepper

1 tablespoon butter

1 teaspoon fresh orange zest

1 teaspoon chopped fresh thyme

1. Pre-heat the air fryer to 400°F.

2. Scrub the carrots and halve them lengthwise. Toss them in the olive oil, season with salt and freshly ground black pepper and transfer to the air fryer.

3. Air-fry at 400°F for 12 minutes, shaking the basket every once in a while to rotate the carrots as they cook.

4. As soon as the carrots have finished cooking, add the butter, orange zest and thyme and toss all the ingredients together in the air fryer basket to melt the butter and coat evenly. Serve warm.

Easy

GF

Veg

Note from Meredith

The timing of this recipe depends on how thick the carrots are. Ideally, 1-inch diameter carrots work well. If your carrots are bigger than 1-inch in diameter, add a couple minutes to the cooking time. Of course, if you can't find heirloom or rainbow carrots, this recipe is just as tasty with regular carrots – just not as pretty.

Per Serving 170 Calories – 8g Fat (4g Sat. Fat) – 15mg Cholesterol – 24g Carbohydrates – 7g Fiber – 11g Sugar – 2g Protein

Parmesan Asparagus

Serves: **2** ■ Temperature: **400˚F** ■ Cooking Time: **5 minutes**

Easy

GF

Veg

1 bunch asparagus, stems trimmed

1 teaspoon olive oil

salt and freshly ground black pepper

¼ cup coarsely grated Parmesan cheese

½ lemon

1. Pre-heat the air fryer to 400°F.

2. Toss the asparagus with the oil and season with salt and freshly ground black pepper.

3. Transfer the asparagus to the air fryer basket and air-fry at 400°F for 5 minutes, shaking the basket to turn the asparagus once or twice during the cooking process.

4. When the asparagus is cooked to your liking, sprinkle the asparagus generously with the Parmesan cheese and close the air fryer drawer again. Let the asparagus sit for 1 minute in the turned-off air fryer. Then, remove the asparagus, transfer it to a serving dish and finish with a grind of black pepper and a squeeze of lemon juice.

Note from Meredith

This recipe is so simple, but sometimes doing very little to good ingredients is all you need to do!

Per Serving 90 Calories – 6g Fat (2.5g Sat. Fat) – 10mg Cholesterol – 5g Carbohydrates – 2g Fiber – 2g Sugar – 7g Protein

Desserts

Peanut Butter Cup Doughnut Holes

Makes: **24 doughnut holes** ■ Temperature: **400°F** ■ Cooking Time: **4 minutes**

1½ cups bread flour

1 teaspoon active dry yeast

1 tablespoon sugar

¼ teaspoon salt

½ cup warm milk

½ teaspoon vanilla extract

2 egg yolks

2 tablespoons melted butter

24 miniature peanut butter cups, plus a few more for garnish

vegetable oil, in a spray bottle

Doughnut Topping

1 cup chocolate chips

2 tablespoons milk

1. Combine the flour, yeast, sugar and salt in a bowl. Add the milk, vanilla, egg yolks and butter. Mix well until the dough starts to come together. Transfer the dough to a floured surface and knead by hand for 2 minutes. Shape the dough into a ball and transfer it to a large oiled bowl. Cover the bowl with a towel and let the dough rise in a warm place for 1 to 1½ hours, until the dough has doubled in size. (See page 61 for a tip on this.)

2. When the dough has risen, punch it down and roll it into a 24-inch long log. Cut the dough into 24 pieces. Push a peanut butter cup into the center of each piece of dough, pinch the dough shut and roll it into a ball. Place the dough balls on a cookie sheet and let them rise in a warm place for 30 minutes.

3. Pre-heat the air fryer to 400°F.

4. Spray or brush the dough balls lightly with vegetable oil. Air-fry eight at a time, at 400°F for 4 minutes, turning them over halfway through the cooking process.

5. While the doughnuts are air frying, prepare the topping. Place the chocolate chips and milk in a microwave safe bowl. Microwave on high for 1 minute. Stir and microwave for an additional 30 seconds if necessary to get all the chips to melt. Stir until the chips are melted and smooth.

6. Dip the top half of the doughnut holes into the melted chocolate. Place them on a rack to set up for just a few minutes and watch them disappear.

Peanut Butter Topping

¼ cup peanut butter

3 tablespoons milk

1 tablespoon powdered sugar

1. Place the peanut butter and milk into a microwave safe bowl. Microwave for 30 seconds. Add the powdered sugar and stir until smooth.

2. Place the peanut butter mixture in a zip lock bag and cut the tip of one corner off to make a small hole. Drizzle thin lines of peanut butter over the chocolate layer on the doughnut holes.

Dress It Up

If you want to decorate these little doughnut holes, you can drizzle a peanut butter topping on in a decorative manner, or chop up a few more peanut butter cups and sprinkle them on top.

Per doughnut hole   150 Calories – 8g Fat (4g Sat. Fat) – 20mg Cholesterol – 19g Carbohydrates – 1g Fiber – 10g Sugar – 3g Protein

Per doughnut hole with peanut butter topping   170 Calories – 9.5g Fat (4g Sat. Fat) – 20mg Cholesterol – 20g Carbohydrates – 1g Fiber – 21g Sugar – 5g Protein

Coconut Crusted Bananas with Pineapple Sauce

Serves: **4** ■ Temperature: **400˚F** ■ Cooking Time: **5 minutes per batch**

Easy

GF*

Pineapple Sauce

1½ cups puréed fresh pineapple

2 tablespoons sugar

juice of 1 lemon

¼ teaspoon ground cinnamon

3 firm bananas

¼ cup sweetened condensed milk

1¼ cups shredded coconut

⅓ cup crushed graham crackers (crumbs)*

vegetable or canola oil, in a spray bottle

vanilla frozen yogurt or ice cream

*Make this recipe gluten free by using gluten-free graham crackers.

1. Make the pineapple sauce by combining the pineapple, sugar, lemon juice and cinnamon in a saucepan. Simmer the mixture on the stovetop for 20 minutes, and then set it aside.

2. Slice the bananas diagonally into ½-inch thick slices and place them in a bowl. Pour the sweetened condensed milk into the bowl and toss the bananas gently to coat. Combine the coconut and graham cracker crumbs together in a shallow dish. Remove the banana slices from the condensed milk and let any excess milk drip off. Dip the banana slices in the coconut and crumb mixture to coat both sides. Spray the coated slices with oil.

3. Pre-heat the air fryer to 400°F.

4. Grease the bottom of the air fryer basket with a little oil. Air-fry the bananas in batches at 400°F for 5 minutes, turning them over halfway through the cooking time. Air-fry until the bananas are golden brown on both sides.

5. Serve warm over vanilla frozen yogurt with some of the pineapple sauce spooned over top.

Note from Meredith
I'm speechless...

Per Serving
Bananas Alone 160 Calories – 4g Fat (2.5g Sat. Fat) – 0mg Cholesterol – 32g Carbohydrates – 3g Fiber – 18g Sugar – 2g Protein
Bananas with Pineapple Sauce 290 Calories – 4g Fat (2.5g Sat. Fat) – 0mg Cholesterol – 48g Carbohydrates – 5g Fiber – 29g Sugar – 3g Protein

S'mores Pockets

Serves: **6** ∎ Temperature: **350˚F** ∎ Cooking Time: **5 minutes per batch**

12 sheets phyllo dough, thawed

1½ cups butter, melted

¾ cup graham cracker crumbs

1 (7-ounce) Giant Hershey's® milk chocolate bar

12 marshmallows, cut in half

1. Place one sheet of the phyllo on a large cutting board. Keep the rest of the phyllo sheets covered with a slightly damp, clean kitchen towel. Brush the phyllo sheet generously with some melted butter. Place a second phyllo sheet on top of the first and brush it with more butter. Repeat with one more phyllo sheet until you have a stack of 3 phyllo sheets with butter brushed between the layers. Cover the phyllo sheets with one quarter of the graham cracker crumbs leaving a 1-inch border on one of the short ends of the rectangle. Cut the phyllo sheets lengthwise into 3 strips.

2. Take 2 of the strips and crisscross them to form a cross with the empty borders at the top and to the left. Place 2 of the chocolate rectangles in the center of the cross. Place 4 of the marshmallow halves on top of the chocolate. Now fold the pocket together by folding the bottom phyllo strip up over the chocolate and marshmallows. Then fold the right side over, then the top strip down and finally the left side over. Brush all the edges generously with melted butter to seal shut. Repeat with the next three sheets of phyllo, until all the sheets have been used. You will be able to make 2 pockets with every second batch because you will have an extra graham cracker crumb strip from the previous set of sheets.

3. Pre-heat the air fryer to 350°F.

4. Transfer 3 pockets at a time to the air fryer basket. Air-fry at 350°F for 4 to 5 minutes, until the phyllo dough is light brown in color. Flip the pockets over halfway through the cooking process. Repeat with the remaining 3 pockets.

5. Serve warm.

Make It Ahead

You can easily prep these pockets ahead of time, holding them in the refrigerator until it is time to air-fry them, OR cook them all the way through and then just re-heat them for 2 minutes at 350°F when you're ready to enjoy!

Per Serving 710 Calories – 50g Fat (30g Sat. Fat) – 105mg Cholesterol – 61g Carbohydrates – 1g Fiber – 30g Sugar – 6g Protein

Hasselback Apple Crisp

Serves: **4** ■ Temperature: **330˚F** ■ Cooking Time: **20 minutes**

GF*

2 large Gala apples, peeled, cored and cut in half

¼ cup butter, melted

½ teaspoon ground cinnamon

2 tablespoons sugar

Topping

3 tablespoons butter, melted

2 tablespoons brown sugar

¼ cup chopped pecans

2 tablespoons rolled oats*

1 tablespoon flour*

vanilla ice cream

caramel sauce

*Make this recipe gluten free by using gluten-free oats and gluten-free flour.

1. Place the apples cut side down on a cutting board. Slicing from stem end to blossom end, make 8 to 10 slits down the apple halves but only slice three quarters of the way through the apple, not all the way through to the cutting board. (See note below for an easy way to do this.)

2. Pre-heat the air fryer to 330°F and pour a little water into the bottom of the air fryer drawer. (This will help prevent the grease that drips into the bottom drawer from burning and smoking.)

3. Transfer the apples to the air fryer basket, flat side down. Combine ¼ cup of melted butter, cinnamon and sugar in a small bowl. Brush this butter mixture onto the apples and air-fry at 330°F for 15 minutes. Baste the apples several times with the butter mixture during the cooking process.

4. While the apples are air-frying, make the filling. Combine 3 tablespoons of melted butter with the brown sugar, pecans, rolled oats and flour in a bowl. Stir with a fork until the mixture resembles small crumbles.

5. When the timer on the air fryer is up, spoon the topping down the center of the apples. Air-fry at 330°F for an additional 5 minutes.

6. Transfer the apples to a serving plate and serve with vanilla ice cream and caramel sauce.

Prep Help

There's an easy way to make the slices for Hasselback apples (or potatoes): place two wooden chopsticks on either side of the apple halves. Slice down and the chopsticks will stop you just in time, preventing you from cutting all the way through the apple.

Per Serving 330 Calories – 24g Fat (12g Sat. Fat) – 50mg Cholesterol – 28g Carbohydrates – 5g Fiber – 18g Sugar – 2g Protein

Annie's Chocolate Chunk Hazelnut Cookies

Makes: **24 cookies** ■ Temperature: **350°F** ■ Cooking Time: **10 to 12 minutes**

Easy

1 cup butter, softened

1 cup brown sugar

½ cup granulated sugar

2 eggs, lightly beaten

1½ teaspoons vanilla extract

1½ cups all-purpose flour

½ cup rolled oats

1 teaspoon baking soda

½ teaspoon salt

2 cups chocolate chunks

½ cup toasted chopped hazelnuts

1. Cream the butter and sugars together until light and fluffy using a stand mixer or electric hand mixer. Add the eggs and vanilla, and beat until well combined.

2. Combine the flour, rolled oats, baking soda and salt in a second bowl. Gradually add the dry ingredients to the wet ingredients with a wooden spoon or spatula. Stir in the chocolate chunks and hazelnuts until distributed throughout the dough.

3. Shape the cookies into small balls about the size of golf balls and place them on a baking sheet. Freeze the cookie balls for at least 30 minutes, or package them in as airtight a package as you can and keep them in your freezer.

4. When you're ready for a delicious snack or dessert, pre-heat the air fryer to 350°F. Cut a piece of parchment paper to fit the number of cookies you are baking. Place the parchment down in the air fryer basket and place the frozen cookie ball or balls on top (remember to leave room for them to expand).

5. Air-fry the cookies at 350°F for 10 to 12 minutes, or until they are done to your liking. Let them cool for a few minutes before enjoying your freshly baked cookie.

Note from Meredith
You'll find that these cookies get quite brown in the air fryer – that's what I like about them! They are dark and crispy on the outside, but inside they are moist and tender and just ooey-gooey good!

Per Cookie 210 Calories – 12g Fat (5g Sat. Fat) – 30mg Cholesterol – 24g Carbohydrates – 1g Fiber – 15g Sugar – 3g Protein

Struffoli

Serves: **so many** ▪ Temperature: **370˚F** ▪ Cooking Time: **20 minutes**

¼ cup butter, softened

⅔ cup sugar

5 eggs

2 teaspoons vanilla extract

zest of 1 lemon

4 cups all-purpose flour

2 teaspoons baking soda

¼ teaspoon salt

16 ounces honey

1 teaspoon ground cinnamon

zest of 1 orange

2 tablespoons water

nonpareils candy sprinkles

1. Cream the butter and sugar together in a bowl until light and fluffy using a hand mixer (or a stand mixer). Add the eggs, vanilla and lemon zest and mix. In a separate bowl, combine the flour, baking soda and salt. Add the dry ingredients to the wet ingredients and mix until you have a soft dough. Shape the dough into a ball, wrap it in plastic and let it rest for 30 minutes.

2. Divide the dough ball into four pieces. Roll each piece into a long rope. Cut each rope into about 25 (½-inch) pieces. Roll each piece into a tight ball. You should have 100 little balls when finished.

3. Pre-heat the air fryer to 370°F.

4. In batches of about 20, transfer the dough balls to the air fryer basket, leaving a small space in between them. Air-fry the dough balls at 370°F for 3 to 4 minutes, shaking the basket when one minute of cooking time remains.

5. After all the dough balls are air-fried, make the honey topping. Melt the honey in a small saucepan on the stovetop. Add the cinnamon, orange zest, and water. Simmer for one minute. Place the air-fried dough balls in a large bowl and drizzle the honey mixture over top. Gently toss to coat all the dough balls evenly. Transfer the coated struffoli to a platter and sprinkle the nonpareil candy sprinkles over top. You can dress the presentation up by piling the balls into the shape of a wreath (see note below) or pile them high in a cone shape to resemble a Christmas tree.

6. Struffoli can be made ahead. Store covered tightly.

Did You Know?
Stuffoli is a traditional Italian dessert made up of small fried balls of dough soaked in honey. They are usually shaped in a wreath or piled up to form a tree. The dessert is considered good luck because the multiple cookie balls are a symbol of abundance. To shape the struffoli into a wreath, grease the outside of a drinking glass and place it on a large round platter. Pile the coated dough balls up around the glass and then sprinkle them with nonpareils. Allow the dough balls to set a little before removing the glass.

Per 4 Pieces 180 Calories – 3g Fat (1.5g Sat. Fat) – 40mg Cholesterol – 35g Carbohydrates – 1g Fiber – 20g Sugar – 3g Protein

Blueberry Cheesecake Tartlets

Makes: **9 tartlets** ■ Temperature: **330°F** ■ Cooking Time: **6 minutes per batch**

Easy

GF*

8 ounces cream cheese, softened

¼ cup sugar

1 egg

½ teaspoon vanilla extract

zest of 2 lemons, divided

9 mini graham cracker tartlet shells*

2 cups blueberries

½ teaspoon ground cinnamon

juice of ½ lemon

¼ cup apricot preserves

*Make this recipe gluten free by making your own tartlet shells with gluten-free graham crackers.

1. Pre-heat the air fryer to 330°F.

2. Combine the cream cheese, sugar, egg, vanilla and the zest of one lemon in a medium bowl and blend until smooth by hand or with an electric hand mixer. Pour the cream cheese mixture into the tartlet shells.

3. Air-fry 3 tartlets at a time at 330°F for 6 minutes, rotating them in the air fryer basket halfway through the cooking time.

4. Combine the blueberries, cinnamon, zest of one lemon and juice of half a lemon in a bowl. Melt the apricot preserves in the microwave or over low heat in a saucepan. Pour the apricot preserves over the blueberries and gently toss to coat.

5. Allow the cheesecakes to cool completely and then top each one with some of the blueberry mixture. Garnish the tartlets with a little sugared lemon peel and refrigerate until you are ready to serve.

Graham Cracker Tartlet Shell

If you can't find pre-made graham cracker tartlet shells, you can make your own graham cracker crust in the bottom of any oven-safe tartlet pan that will fit into the air fryer. Combine 1 cup crushed graham cracker crumbs, ¼ cup sugar and 6 tablespoons melted butter in a bowl and then press this mixture into the bottom of your tart pans.

Per Serving 220 Calories – 12g Fat (7g Sat. Fat) – 50mg Cholesterol – 25g Carbohydrates – 1g Fiber – 16g Sugar – 3g Protein

Sugared Pizza Dough Dippers
with Raspberry Cream Cheese Dip

Serves: **10 to 15** ■ Temperature: **350°F** ■ Cooking Time: **8 minutes per batch**

1 pound pizza dough*

½ cup butter, melted

¾ to 1 cup sugar

Raspberry Cream Cheese Dip

4 ounces cream cheese, softened

2 tablespoons powdered sugar

½ teaspoon almond extract or almond paste

1½ tablespoons milk

¼ cup raspberry preserves

fresh raspberries

*Make this recipe gluten free by using a gluten-free pizza dough mix.

1. If you would like to make your own dough, follow the recipe on page 61 (dough primer page). Cut the ingredients in half or save half of the dough for another recipe.

2. When you're ready to make your sugared dough dippers, remove your pizza dough from the refrigerator at least 1 hour prior to baking and let it sit on the counter, covered gently with plastic wrap.

3. Roll the dough into two 15-inch logs. Cut each log into 20 slices and roll each slice so that it is 3- to 3½-inches long. Cut each slice in half and twist the dough halves together 3 to 4 times. Place the twisted dough on a cookie sheet, brush with melted butter and sprinkle sugar over the dough twists.

4. Pre-heat the air fryer to 350°F.

5. Brush the bottom of the air fryer basket with a little melted butter. Air-fry the dough twists in batches. Place 8 to 12 (depending on the size of your air fryer) in the air fryer basket.

6. Air-fry for 6 minutes. Turn the dough strips over and brush the other side with butter. Air-fry for an additional 2 minutes.

7. While the dough twists are cooking, make the cream cheese and raspberry dip. Whip the cream cheese with a hand mixer until fluffy. Add the powdered sugar, almond extract and milk, and beat until smooth. Fold in the raspberry preserves and transfer to a serving dish.

8. As the batches of dough twists are complete, place them into a shallow dish. Brush with more melted butter and generously coat with sugar, shaking the dish to cover both sides. Serve the sugared dough dippers warm with the raspberry cream cheese dip on the side. Garnish with fresh raspberries.

Your Favorite Berry
You can easily swap out the raspberry preserves for blackberry, blueberry, strawberry or peach preserves if you're in the mood for something different.

Per Serving
Dough Dippers 190 Calories – 8g Fat (4.5g Sat. Fat) – 20mg Cholesterol – 28g Carbohydrates – 0g Fiber – 12g Sugar – 3g Protein
Dough Dippers with Raspberry Cream Cheese Dip 250 Calories – 11.5g Fat (6.5g Sat. Fat) – 30mg Cholesterol – 34g Carbohydrates – 0g Fiber – 17g Sugar – 4g Protein

Black and Blue Clafoutis

Serves: **2 (6-inch) desserts, serves 4** ■ Temperature: **320˚F** ■ Cooking Time: **30 minutes (12 to 15 minutes per batch)**

Easy

GF*

6-inch pie pan

3 large eggs

½ cup sugar

1 teaspoon vanilla extract

2 tablespoons butter, melted

1 cup milk

½ cup all-purpose flour*

1 cup blackberries

1 cup blueberries

2 tablespoons confectioners' sugar

*Make this recipe gluten free by using gluten-free flour.

1. Pre-heat the air fryer to 320°F.

2. Combine the eggs and sugar in a bowl and whisk vigorously until smooth, lighter in color and well combined. Add the vanilla extract, butter and milk and whisk together well. Add the flour and whisk just until no lumps or streaks of white remain.

3. Scatter half the blueberries and blackberries in a greased (6-inch) pie pan or cake pan. Pour half of the batter (about 1¼ cups) on top of the berries and transfer the tart pan to the air fryer basket. You can use an aluminum foil sling to help with this by taking a long piece of aluminum foil, folding it in half lengthwise twice until it is roughly 26-inches by 3-inches. Place this under the pie dish and hold the ends of the foil to move the pie dish in and out of the air fryer basket. Tuck the ends of the foil beside the pie dish while it cooks in the air fryer.

4. Air-fry at 320°F for 12 to 15 minutes or until the clafoutis has puffed up and is still a little jiggly in the center. Remove the clafoutis from the air fryer, invert it onto a plate and let it cool while you bake the second batch. Serve the clafoutis warm (not hot), dusted with confectioners' sugar on top.

Did You Know?
Clafoutis is a simple French dessert with a batter similar to crêpe batter, so when cooked, it is like a puffy fruity pancake. It puffs up in the air fryer and then falls as it cools. Not to worry – it's just as delicious! It's most often made with cherries, but I use blackberries and blueberries here. You can use any berry you like.

Per Serving 340 Calories – 11g Fat (6g Sat. Fat) – 160mg Cholesterol – 53g Carbohydrates – 3g Fiber – 38g Sugar – 9g Protein

Midnight Nutella® Banana Sandwich

Serves: **2** ■ Temperature: **370˚F** ■ Cooking Time: **8 minutes**

butter, softened

4 slices white bread*

¼ cup chocolate hazelnut spread (Nutella®)

1 banana

*Make this recipe gluten free by using gluten-free bread.

1. Pre-heat the air fryer to 370°F.

2. Spread the softened butter on one side of all the slices of bread and place the slices buttered side down on the counter. Spread the chocolate hazelnut spread on the other side of the bread slices. Cut the banana in half and then slice each half into three slices lengthwise. Place the banana slices on two slices of bread and top with the remaining slices of bread (buttered side up) to make two sandwiches. Cut the sandwiches in half (triangles or rectangles) – this will help them all fit in the air fryer at once. Transfer the sandwiches to the air fryer.

3. Air-fry at 370°F for 5 minutes. Flip the sandwiches over and air-fry for another 2 to 3 minutes, or until the top bread slices are nicely browned. Pour yourself a glass of milk or a midnight nightcap while the sandwiches cool slightly and enjoy!

Easy

GF*

Perfect Accompaniment
These decadent simple treats are a perfect midnight snack and are especially tasty with a little nip of Grand Marnier®. You can make many variations on this sandwich by substituting other ingredients for the bananas – try raspberries, strawberries or even slices of ripe peach.

Per Serving 430 Calories – 21g Fat (9g Sat. Fat) – 20mg Cholesterol – 57g Carbohydrates – 4g Fiber – 31g Sugar – 6g Protein

Pear and Almond Biscotti Crumble

Serves: **6** ■ Temperature: **350˚F** ■ Cooking Time: **65 minutes**

Easy

7-inch cake pan or ceramic dish

3 pears, peeled, cored and sliced

½ cup brown sugar

¼ teaspoon ground ginger

1 teaspoon ground cinnamon

⅛ teaspoon ground nutmeg

2 tablespoons cornstarch

1¼ cups (4 to 5) almond biscotti, coarsely crushed

¼ cup all-purpose flour

¼ cup sliced almonds

¼ cup butter, melted

1. Combine the pears, brown sugar, ginger, cinnamon, nutmeg and cornstarch in a bowl. Toss to combine and then pour the pear mixture into a greased 7-inch cake pan or ceramic dish.

2. Combine the crushed biscotti, flour, almonds and melted butter in a medium bowl. Toss with a fork until the mixture resembles large crumbles. Sprinkle the biscotti crumble over the pears and cover the pan with aluminum foil.

3. Pre-heat the air fryer to 350°F.

4. Air-fry at 350°F for 60 minutes. Remove the aluminum foil and air-fry for an additional 5 minutes to brown the crumble layer.

5. Serve warm with vanilla ice cream or whipped cream.

Substitution Tip

Using almond biscotti is a great change from the crisp topping you may be used to. If you can't find almond biscotti, you can use plain biscotti and add more almonds OR you can substitute with almond cookies.

Per Serving 330 Calories – 15g Fat (6g Sat. Fat) – 35mg Cholesterol – 47g Carbohydrates – 5g Fiber – 27g Sugar – 5g Protein

Air-Fried Strawberry Hand Tarts

Makes: **9 tarts** ▪ Temperature: **350˚F** ▪ Cooking Time: **9 minutes per batch**

½ cup butter, softened

½ cup sugar

2 eggs

1 teaspoon vanilla extract

2 tablespoons lemon zest

2½ cups all-purpose flour

1 teaspoon baking powder

¼ teaspoon salt

1¼ cups strawberry jam, divided

1 egg white, beaten

1 cup powdered sugar

2 teaspoons milk

1. Combine the butter and sugar in a bowl and beat with an electric mixer until the mixture is light and fluffy. Add the eggs one at a time. Add the vanilla extract and lemon zest and mix well. In a separate bowl, combine the flour, baking powder and salt. Add the dry ingredients to the wet ingredients, mixing just until the dough comes together. Transfer the dough to a floured surface and knead by hand for 10 minutes. Cover with a clean kitchen towel and let the dough rest for 30 minutes. (Alternatively, dough can be mixed and kneaded in a stand mixer.)

2. Divide the dough in half and roll each half out into a ¼-inch thick rectangle that measures 12-inches x 9-inches. Cut each rectangle of dough into nine 4-inch x 3-inch rectangles (a pizza cutter is very helpful for this task). You should have 18 rectangles. Spread two teaspoons of strawberry jam in the center of nine of the rectangles leaving a ¼-inch border around the edges. Brush the egg white around the edges of each rectangle and top with the remaining nine rectangles of dough. Press the back of a fork around the edges to seal the tarts shut. Brush the top of the tarts with the beaten egg white and pierce the dough three or four times down the center of the tart with a fork.

3. Pre-heat the air fryer to 350°F.

4. Air-fry the tarts in batches at 350°F for 6 minutes. Flip the tarts over and air-fry for an additional 3 minutes.

5. While the tarts are air-frying, make the icing. Combine the powdered sugar, ¼ cup strawberry preserves and milk in a bowl, whisking until the icing is smooth. Spread the icing over the top of each tart, leaving an empty border around the edges. Decorate with sprinkles if desired.

Per Tart 420 Calories – 12g Fat (7g Sat. Fat) – 70mg Cholesterol – 73g Carbohydrates – 1g Fiber – 39g Sugar – 6g Protein

Air-Fried Beignets

Makes: **24 beignets** ■ Temperature: **350°F** ■ Cooking Time: **5 minutes per batch**

¾ cup lukewarm water (about 90°F)

¼ cup sugar

1 generous teaspoon active dry yeast (½ envelope)

3½ to 4 cups all-purpose flour

½ teaspoon salt

2 tablespoons unsalted butter, room temperature and cut into small pieces

1 egg, lightly beaten

½ cup evaporated milk

¼ cup melted butter

1 cup confectioners' sugar

chocolate sauce or raspberry sauce, to dip

1. Combine the lukewarm water, a pinch of the sugar and the yeast in a bowl and let it proof for 5 minutes. It should froth a little. If it doesn't froth, your yeast is not active and you should start again with new yeast.

2. Combine 3½ cups of the flour, salt, 2 tablespoons of butter and the remaining sugar in a large bowl, or in the bowl of a stand mixer. Add the egg, evaporated milk and yeast mixture to the bowl and mix with a wooden spoon (or the paddle attachment of the stand mixer) until the dough comes together in a sticky ball. Add a little more flour if necessary to get the dough to form. Transfer the dough to an oiled bowl, cover with plastic wrap or a clean kitchen towel and let it rise in a warm place for at least 2 hours or until it has doubled in size. Longer is better for flavor development and you can even let the dough rest in the refrigerator overnight (just remember to bring it to room temperature before proceeding with the recipe).

3. Roll the dough out to ½-inch thickness. Cut the dough into rectangular or diamond-shaped pieces. You can make the beignets any size you like, but this recipe will give you 24 (2-inch x 3-inch) rectangles.

4. Pre-heat the air fryer to 350°F.

5. Brush the beignets on both sides with some of the melted butter and air-fry in batches at 350°F for 5 minutes, turning them over halfway through if desired. (They will brown on all sides without being flipped, but flipping them will brown them more evenly.)

6. As soon as the beignets are finished, transfer them to a plate or baking sheet and dust with the confectioners' sugar. Serve warm with a chocolate or raspberry sauce.

Dress It Up
To make a super easy and quick raspberry sauce, stir ¼ cup of raspberry jam together with 1 tablespoon of warm water. Thin it just to the consistency you like for dipping. Et voilà!

Per Beignet 130 Calories – 3.5g Fat (2g Sat. Fat) – 15mg Cholesterol – 22g Carbohydrates – 1g Fiber – 7g Sugar – 3g Protein

Index

Meredith's Cookbooks

Air Fry Everything!

Air Fry Everything! was a 2016 best-seller, selling over 200,000 copies. This cookbook will take your air-frying to the next level, creating delicious food and quick meals that burst with flavor, texture and color without the added calories and fat. *Air Fry Everything!* offers 140 all new recipes for both novices and experts, along with air-frying tips, tricks and techniques.

Fast Favorites Under Pressure

Fast Favorites Under Pressure offers over 120 recipes, tips and tricks to help you be successful with your 4-quart pressure cooker. With recipes for soups, pastas, meats and seafood, grains, vegetarian entrées and desserts, there's a way for every eater to get a meal on the table in a fraction of the time.

Delicious Under Pressure

Delicious Under Pressure was one of 2015's best-selling cookbooks. It is full of easy, flavorful, and unexpected pressure cooker recipes. With 131 recipes, over 110 photos and all new chapters on Vegetarian Main Courses and Breakfast Dishes, it's a must-have cookbook for pressure-cooking at any level.

Comfortable Under Pressure

If your pressure cooker has been collecting dust, then you need to get Comfortable Under Pressure! With 125 recipes and over 100 tips and explanations, Blue Jean Chef: Comfortable Under Pressure will help you create delicious meals while becoming more versatile and at ease with your pressure cooker.

Comfortable in the Kitchen

Are you as comfortable in the kitchen as you are in your blue jeans? In Blue Jean Chef: Comfortable in the Kitchen, Meredith helps you settle into your comfort zone in the kitchen with 200 kitchen-tested recipes, tips, tricks and explanations of cooking techniques. Each chapter contains basic recipes that will give you a solid understanding of how the dish works, and four other recipes that build on that technique, but use different ingredients to create a unique and delicious meal.

Air Fryer Cooking Chart

NOTE: All times and temperatures below assume that the food is flipped over half way through the cooking time or the basket is shaken to redistribute ingredients once or twice.

Vegetables

	Temperature (°F)	Time (min)		Temperature (°F)	Time (min)
Asparagus (sliced 1-inch)	400°F	5	Onions (sliced)	400°F	15
Beets (whole)	400°F	40	Parsnips (½-inch chunks)	380°F	15
Broccoli (florets)	400°F	6	Peppers (1-inch chunks)	400°F	15
Brussels Sprouts (halved)	380°F	15	Potatoes (small baby, 1½ lbs)	400°F	15
Carrots (sliced ½-inch)	380°F	15	Potatoes (1-inch chunks)	400°F	12
Cauliflower (florets)	400°F	12	Potatoes (baked whole)	400°F	40
Corn on the cob	390°F	6	Spaghetti Squash (halved)	370°F	30
Eggplant (1½-inch cubes)	400°F	15	Squash (½-inch chunks)	400°F	12
Fennel (quartered)	370°F	15	Sweet Potato (baked)	380°F	30 to 35
Green Beans	400°F	5	Sweet Potato (1-inch chunks)	400°F	20
Kale leaves	250°F	12	Tomatoes (cherry)	400°F	4
Mushrooms (sliced ¼-inch)	400°F	5	Tomatoes (halves)	350°F	10
Onions (pearl)	400°F	10	Zucchini (½-inch sticks)	400°F	12

Chicken

	Temperature (°F)	Time (min)		Temperature (°F)	Time (min)
Breasts, bone in (1¼ lbs.)	370°F	25	Legs, bone in (1¾ lbs.)	380°F	30
Breasts, boneless (4 oz.)	380°F	12	Wings (2 lbs.)	400°F	12
Breasts, stuffed	350°F	14	Game Hen (halved - 2 lbs.)	390°F	20
Drumsticks (2½ lbs.)	370°F	20	Whole Chicken (6½ lbs.)	360°F	75
Thighs, bone in (2 lbs.)	380°F	22	Tenders	360°F	8 to 10
Thighs, boneless (1½ lbs.)	380°F	18 to 20	Turkey Breast (whole, bone-in, 3 lbs.)	350°F	35 to 45

	Temperature (°F)	Time (min)		Temperature (°F)	Time (min)
Beef					
Burger (4 oz.)	370°F	16 to 20	Meatloaf (3 lbs.)	350°F	45 to 50
Filet Mignon (8 oz.)	400°F	18	Ribeye, bone in (1-inch, 8 oz.)	400°F	10 to15
Flank Steak (1½ lbs.)	400°F	12	Sirloin steaks (1-inch, 12 oz.)	400°F	9 to 14
London Broil (2 lbs.)	400°F	20 to 28	Beef Eye Round Roast (4 lbs.)	390°F	45 to 55
Meatballs (1-inch)	380°F	7	Veal Chops (bone-in, 6 oz.)	400°F	10 to 15
Meatballs (3-inch)	380°F	10			

	Temperature (°F)	Time (min)		Temperature (°F)	Time (min)
Pork and Lamb					
Loin (2 lbs.)	360°F	55	Bacon (thick cut)	400°F	6 to 10
Pork Chops, bone in (1-inch, 6 oz.)	400°F	12	Sausages	380°F	15
Pork Chops, boneless (1-inch)	400°F	12	Lamb Loin Chops (1-inch thick)	400°F	8 to 12
Tenderloin (1 lb.)	370°F	15	Lollipop Lamb Chops	400°F	7
Bacon (regular)	400°F	5 to 7	Rack of lamb (1½ - 2 lbs.)	380°F	22

	Temperature (°F)	Time (min)		Temperature (°F)	Time (min)
Fish and Seafood					
Calamari (8 oz.)	400°F	4	Tuna steak	400°F	7 to 10
Fish Fillet (1-inch, 8 oz.)	400°F	10	Crab Cake (4 oz.)	400°F	10
Salmon, fillet (6 oz.)	380°F	12	Lobster Tail (6 oz.)	370°F	5
Swordfish steak	400°F	10	Scallops	400°F	5 to 7
			Shrimp	400°F	5

	Temperature (°F)	Time (min)		Temperature (°F)	Time (min)
Frozen Foods					
Onion Rings (12 oz.)	400°F	8	Egg rolls	400°F	12
Thin French Fries (20 oz.)	400°F	14	Fish Sticks (10 oz.)	400°F	10
Thick French Fries (17 oz.)	400°F	18	Fish Fillets (½-inch, 10 oz.)	400°F	14
Mozzarella Sticks (11 oz.)	400°F	8	Chicken Nuggets (12 oz.)	400°F	10
Pot Stickers (10 oz.)	400°F	8	Breaded Shrimp	400°F	9

About the Author

Meredith Laurence grew up in Canada with a British mother and a Trinidadian father who both loved food and exploring cuisines from around the world. Meredith learned the same at a very young age and the rest has been history!

Now known as the Blue Jean Chef, Meredith has worked in the food world for over 20 years. After graduating from the New England Culinary Institute, she worked as a line cook at two Michelin-rated restaurants in France, as well as at the renowned Zuni Café in San Francisco and at Café Rouge in Berkeley, California. Meredith then went on to work as a culinary instructor, a food product consultant and as a test kitchen manager. She now works as the Blue Jean Chef on live television doing cooking demonstrations, giving viewers advice on cooking and equipping their kitchens.

Meredith is a best-selling author, with over 650,000 books sold to date. In addition to her cookbook writing and appearances on television, Meredith also writes and appears in a cooking series called The Basics, which can be seen on YouTube (www.youtube.com/bluejeanchef). In over 100 episodes of The Basics, Meredith takes viewers through a series of easy cooking techniques and recipes, empowering even the most novice cook.

She splits her time between Canada and Pennsylvania, where she and her partner enjoy their dogs, playing golf, skiing, cooking together at home and exploring the restaurant scene wherever they find themselves.

Stay Connected with Meredith

Check out her **website** for more recipes and techniques: www.bluejeanchef.com

Like her on **Facebook:** www.facebook.com/bluejeanchef

Follow her on **Twitter:** www.twitter.com/bluejeanchef

Follow her on **Instagram:** www.instagram.com/bluejeanchef

Visit her on **Pinterest:** www.pinterest.com/bluejeanchef